Dreams and Delusions

Dreams and Delusions

The Impact of Romantic Fantasy on Women

Mari Hanes

BANTAM BOOKS
New York • Toronto • London • Sydney • Auckland

DREAMS AND DELUSIONS
A Bantam Book / August 1991

"Imaginary Lovers" recorded by Atlanta Rhythm Section,
used by permission of the Lowery Group.

"Faithless Heart" recorded by Amy Grant, used by
permission of Bug and Bear Company.

"Big Time" by Stormie and Michael Omartian, used by
permission of Word Records.

Library of Congress Cataloging-in-Publication Data
Hanes, Mari.
    Dreams and delusions : the impact of romantic
fantasy on women / Mari Hanes.
        p.   cm.
    Includes bibliographical references and index.
    ISBN 0-553-35338-1
    1. Women—United States—Psychology.   2. Sexual
fantasies—United States.   3. Imagery (Psychology).
I. Title.   II. Title: Romantic fantasy on women.
HQ1206.H2393   1991
305.4—dc20   90-26223
                                                   CIP

Published simultaneously in the United States and Canada

Bantam Books are published by Bantam Books, a division of
Bantam Doubleday Dell Publishing Group, Inc. Its
trademark, consisting of the words "Bantam Books" and the
portrayal of a rooster, is Registered in U.S. Patent and
Trademark Office and in other countries. Marca Registrada.
Bantam Books, 666 Fifth Avenue, New York, New York
10103.

PRINTED IN THE UNITED STATES OF AMERICA

FFG   0   9   8   7   6   5   4   3   2   1

For Cliff,
the Love of my life.

Table of Contents

Preface

Dear Mari,

I know that I should be a very happy woman.

I have been married for eight years and I have a healthy little boy and a baby girl. My husband, Tom, is a good father and a good provider. He has worked hard so that we could purchase our first home, but he still makes time to be with me and the children. Tom and I go to church together, have common interests, and we hardly ever fight.

In spite of all of this, I am not as happy as I expected to be. I have not been content or satisfied; I have had the nagging feeling that I was missing out on something. . . . I kept longing for more romance.

Until I heard you teach on "The Fortress of Your Mind," I had never connected my discontentment with the things I imagine. I had never realized that I have been living with subtle lies about romance. My daydreams had become delusions. I didn't know that I was asking my husband to measure up to a mirage.

I just wanted to say thank you . . . My new understanding of spiritual warfare as it applies to everyday home life is the key to my true happiness. And in the long run, I believe, it will save both my marriage and my sanity.

Sincerely,
one of your sisters,
Rene

Rene's letter is an echo of hundreds of letters that I have received. An incredible number of modern women have said, "I am not as happy or content in marriage as I expected to be, and I keep longing for more romance."

I have complete empathy for Rene and for the tens of thousands like her: we are all a product of "the great American fantasy machine."

I was fifteen when I discovered the joy of gothic romance novels. I read my way over a mountain of current paperbacks and on to the heights of classics such as *Tristan and Isolde*.

I was also part of the first generation of Americans truly born and bred on that great fantasy machine called television. As a preschooler, I poured tea for my dolls and toy animals while "As the World Turns" and other original soaps droned on in the background. When I was in grade school, television was the only babysitter my mom could afford when the flu or measles kept me at home and pillowed on the couch. I quickly grew to love the old movies that filled the afternoon time slots—those black-and-white films of the forties that were unashamedly romantic.

And I am part of the first large middle class ever bombarded from birth by the arsenal of modern advertisers. Remember the commercial where the beautiful young couple, both dressed in white, sipped Coca-Cola on the deck of their sailboat and drifted into a Caribbean sunset? Well, that one went deep into my romantic psyche.

In high school and college, I was known to emerge from films like *The Great Gatsby* with a nose that could have won a Rudolph-the-Reindeer contest. I'll admit it, I have always been a pushover for tearjerkers.

Then there are the songs: I love every kind of music, and lyrics automatically implanted themselves in my mind. From the words being sung, I realized that I was not the only young woman whose romantic imagination was on overdrive.

It was no wonder, then, that I and the majority of female

Preface

Americans of today's generation reached adulthood with quite a bit of extra *emotional baggage*—two oversized suitcases, a garment bag, and assorted hand-held carryons filled with an entourage of imaginary lovers.

In 1982, I began a survey which would eventually include almost 10,000 women, a survey designed to look at the impact the media deluge of romantic and sexual fantasy has had on the hearts and minds of modern women. This book is written in response to that survey and to the questions that women have asked. It is also written in response to other books—to best-sellers that encourage women to "pull out all the stops on their sexual and romantic fantasies" and to *The Cinderella Complex,* a fine book by Colette Dowling which calls on women to face reality.

In *The Cinderella Complex,* Ms. Dowling concludes that sooner or later every woman will see "the existential terror that confronts us all." I do not write from an existential world view, but rather from a Christian world view. I do this without apology. When confronted by a world view of "existential terror," a world view of faith is the only alternative. And faith has a positive impact on our view of sexuality because sexuality is not purely physical but also emotional and deeply spiritual.

This book has not been written from a straitlaced mentality that opposes the human imagination and the role of the imagination in sexuality. I simply share the concern expressed by the great author C. S. Lewis a generation ago: "I view the imagination as mankind's crowning glory. My concern is that, from the input we receive in the twentieth century, romance may be the *only* way the individual ever uses that imagination."

This book is also written with a great deal of hope. It is written with the hope that, like Rene whose letter I quoted, many women will discover growing happiness and contentment *not just in fantasy, but in reality.*

Chapter One

The Great American Fantasy Machine

"Imaginary lovers will never let you down—
Imaginary lovers are always around . . ."

THE words pounding from the car stereo were loud and crystal clear. Sitting in my car, waiting in a long line with other mothers who were also performing the daily ritual of picking up children at the door of the kindergarten, I had absentmindedly switched on the radio. This song was new to me, so I listened closely as the words came again—"Imaginary lovers are always around."

These were not simply lyrics, but a modern American philosophy, set to a tune that would keep the song running through my head all day. Like anyone else who was listening, I was being exposed to the allure of "imaginary lovers," an allure that permeates today's media-oriented society. Today we are constantly tempted to open the door of our minds to invisible partners, who we hope will meet our insatiable need for romance.

The human imagination is our greatest treasure. With it, we "see things that are not as though they were." We compose symphonies; we write classic literature; we develop new inventions; we push back the frontiers of modern medicine. Our ability to dream and create flows from God who formed man in His image.

The imagination is also an important component of human sexuality, and each of us has romantic and sexual fantasies. No human relationship can begin, not one word can be spoken, unless first conceived in the mind.

But should the awesome force of the individual human imagination be focused on daydreams and romantic fantasy? How does one's thought-life affect happiness and overall emotional wholeness? Does today's generation of women define love differently from women in the past? What does continual exposure to "romantic fantasies" do to the long-term health of a marriage?

These are vital questions—vital because there has never been a time when the average woman was more pressed toward fantasy, daydreams, and emotional adventure. *A deluge of fantasy inundates modern life.*

THE DELUGE

In the early seventies, *The Sensuous Man* and *The Sensuous Woman* hit the national best-seller list and stayed there for months, beginning a trend in sexual advice books. Read by millions, such books give hints for using the imagination to put zest and "romance" back into a marriage. Here is one hint that is given:

A husband should have his wife dress up like a woman of the streets and wait for him on a downtown corner. He should meet her and "pick her up," each pretending throughout the evening that the other is a stranger.

The basic idea of using imagination and mental games (although not as extreme as in the previous example) is widely

accepted. It is even taught at the beginning of marriage en-
richment seminars by many highly esteemed professional counselors. At this time in our culture, we are tremendously
influenced by forces that say *"Set your imagination completely free."*
We are pushed to mentally develop our fantasies. We are told,
"Your daydreams are your own business; you need not control them."

A basic premise of this modern thinking is that uninhibited
erotic fantasy with imaginary lovers cannot hurt you. In fact,
many counselors say it even helps you, because you are working
through erotic feelings inwardly.

In an appearance on Phil Donahue's show, the husband-
and-wife team who wrote *Fantasy Will Set You Free* talked
about their elaborate role-playing encounters. They spoke
about the use of sexual aids and soft porn as "marriage en-
hancers."

"Physically, I am with my husband," the wife said with a
smile, "but mentally, I have never been with the same man
twice!"

The mass media bombards modern men and women with
suggestions for erotic fantasy, daydreams, and emotional experiences. Dorothy Corkille Briggs is a psychologist and
teacher who specializes in the thought-life and self-esteem of
Americans, especially young people. She says, "Today, sex
receives exaggerated attention. . . . Now, *sex as recreation* is continually thrust at us from all directions: advertisements, television, movies, novels, art, even clothing styles. Modern
technology is flooding our minds with sexual input."

LOVE ACCORDING TO THE CAMERA LENS

The flood of sexual input fills our vision hour after hour on
television. In a recent *TV Guide*, we read listings and advertisements such as:

This week's cable rerun of FANTASY ISLAND is the story of Delia Janssen, midwest school teacher who meets the lover of her steamy fantasies—in person.

Watch FANTASY LOVER Monday night at 8:00 p.m. A CBS movie premiere. He stole her diary, and seduced her by making her romantic fantasies come true.

And the synopsis of just five days' events on a popular soap opera makes the mind swirl:

Outside a bar, a car veers and misses Siobhan. Siobhan accuses Max, who insists he is innocent. Both are stunned to feel an intense attraction, and she quickly leaves. Max is angered by Jacqueline's return to help him through his trial. Ryan unsuccessfully tries to reunite Jack and Leigh. Jack forbids Ryan to see Rick. Tiger tells Maggie she needs a makeover. Dave, angered that Tiger will do anything Rick suggests in order to be a star, invites Kate to the Ball. Frank and Jill make love, but agree not to tell the family that they have reconciled. . . .

One soap opera executive told *TV Guide,* "In prime-time TV, we cater to middle-aged women viewers, so we've capitulated wholeheartedly to the young-hunk phenomenon. We have roles for a dozen clones of Mel Gibson, Matt Dillon, and Richard Gere—every day we want our show to tingle with the body heat Gere produced in the movie *Breathless.* (Although soap executives say they cater to middle-aged viewers, 80 percent of high school girls surveyed in New York State admit to watching at least one soap opera faithfully each day after school.)

Television's fantasies are echoed by the advertising industry, which endeavors to put sexual steam into even a single-scene ad. High over Times Square in New York City, a tightly muscled athlete reclines seductively in his white briefs; this looming forty-eight-foot billboard for Calvin Klein seems to sell everything but cotton. Not to be outdone, the Jockey company turns our latest sports heroes into pinup men. In bookstores from Tallahassee to Tucson, "Hunk A-Month" calendars reproducing these ads are sold out long before the cheesecake competition.

In this world of mass advertising, even toothpaste, deodorant, and denture cream are sold by sex appeal. "Let's face it," stated an advertising expert, "our motto has become 'SELL WITH SIZZLE.'"

All of this sexual input cannot help but become "food for thought," making this generation of women different from women in generations past. After all, how many *acts of seduction* did your grandmother see as she was maturing? (I asked my own grandmother, and it was a grand total of *none*.) How about you? The answer will depend on your age and whether or not you watched much television as a child. Now, how many acts of seduction and violence will your children see? Hundreds. Maybe even thousands!

Changes in input and ideas since the nineteenth century have been studied by Frances Cogan, associate professor at the University of Oregon. In her book *All-American Girl: The Ideal of Real Womanhood in Mid-nineteenth Century America,* Dr. Cogan presents advice offered to women by the Dear Abbys of the last century. She believes that a lot of old-fashioned counsel like the following would be well-taken today: "Pure sentimentality—love at first sight in the moonlight with a 'Prince on a White Horse'—has a high and deadly price. Beware the philanderer, the good-looking man with such vanity in excess that it renders him a mere shell of humanity."

Dr. Cogan notes that toward the turn of the century, advice and women's thinking began to change. There was more emphasis on romance, which took on an almost ethereal aspect, and at the same time women were "snookered" into feeling they should lean on men and adopt a "fading flower" attitude. "*It was the beginning of brainwashing,*" Cogan says. "And what's worse, many romantic script writers are brainwashing us today with an even more ethereal picture of what we should expect from romance."

ON THE SILVER SCREEN

In the 1980s, there was a marked trend in the film industry toward the pursuit of fantasy. *The Thief of Hearts, Mannequin,* and *Body Heat* are only a few of the films in which characters' lives are ruled by sexual fantasy. In the highly acclaimed *Broadcast News,* the leading actress meets a man who looks like one she's imagined and then faces heartbreak when she cannot mold him to her specifications. In *The Witches of Eastwick,* three women are so obsessed with their fantasies that they actually try to conjure up a man to make them come true, and end up battling the demonic.

We are not just affected by movies with such obvious themes; we are also subtly affected by the "perfection" of the stars on the screen. When Robert Redford kisses Meryl Streep in *Out of Africa,* for example, the lighting is soft, the music is moving, and both stars have spent hours with the makeup artists. The camera works its magic, and viewers are swept away into the mirage.

The message that is presented by filmmakers time and time again is that *the entire goal of life is to be involved in passionate pursuit, emotional turmoil, and final sexual conquest.*

Joy Davidson, a psychotherapist in private practice in Beverly Hills, California, has this interesting comment on the effect that this era of filmmaking may be having on women:

> Sensation-seeking (the drive to seek varied, novel, and complex situations and experiences, coupled with the willingness to take risks in order to find them) is a *potentially healthy* personality trait. Historically, though, women have

not been provided access to the same healthy outlets for excitement-seeking as men have. Women have been subtly taught to meet their sensation-seeking needs *through their relationships* or their emotional lives.

In film drama, women are mostly virtuous victims who need to be rescued, or ladies gone wrong, absorbed in the challenges of wooing, rescuing, or—in the hard action shows—destroying a difficult man. Women and girls who are watching receive strong but deceptive instruction about seeking excitement and meaning: *"Get it with a man, through a man, or by repeatedly rebelling against the man you are closest to."*

Through the magic of the motion picture, modern women have done so much vicarious living that they may find it difficult to separate a romantic mirage from love in reality. "I have seen so many love stories at the theater," confided a Los Angeles movie critic, "that reality is beginning to seem like just another story, and I watch myself acting out the parts."

THE MESSAGE OF MUSIC

The American fantasy machine also calls to us hauntingly from the lyrics of just about every variety of twentieth-century music:

- Glen Campbell sang the country ballad about the day-dreams of the everyday housewife.
- Simon and Garfunkel sang that all the girls they knew when they were single couldn't ever match their sweet imagination.
- Charley Pride sang that all women get lonely and often a daydream is all they have.
- Billy Joel sang that sometimes a sexual fantasy is all you need.

• And, of course, there's the song mentioned at the beginning of this chapter which talked about the "imaginary lovers who will never let you down."

Hard rock records and rap tunes are even more graphic; one song repeats the blatant phrase "Do it in your imagination." Olivia Newton-John croons about her fantasies and says, "Let's Get Physical." And various songs all called "Fantasy" have been recorded by such groups as Aldo Nova, Alabama, and Earth, Wind & Fire. On NBC's "Tonight Show" with Johnny Carson, actress Bernadette Peters sang a ballad in support of imaginary lovers and masturbation—a song with the message that when one cannot make love with another, one can still make love alone.

Music historians point out that in previous generations songs were written about a wide variety of human experiences. The folk music of every nation brings us messages of how people felt about their land, their work, their family relationships, the wonders of nature, their struggles to survive. Yes, there were wonderful songs about the love between men and women—but these were balanced by songs about other aspects of the human experience.

Today, 95 out of every 100 popular songs recorded deal *solely* with the male-female relationship, and specifically sexual attraction, chronicling new love, old love, or love gone wrong. Thematically, modern music is incredibly one-track and, in light of the history of music, unbalanced.

How are we affected by the pervasiveness of this theme? Psychotherapist Joy Davidson comments: "Many powerful lessons about womanhood are learned through models of femininity that reach women from all sides—magazines, movies, advertisements, and songs. It is through these seemingly 'lightweight' sources that they come to grasp some exceptionally *heavyweight messages about what it means to be a woman and, most importantly, how to be a woman.*"

One doesn't even decide to memorize the words of a song; a rhymed message set to music is one of the easiest things to recall. While today's woman is shopping, while she is exercising at a sports club—or while she waits in the car to pick up her children from school—songs played in the background pass with ease into her memory.

In the words of the master Austrian composer Joseph Haydn, "Whatever is set to music, the masses will remember."

THE POWER OF PRINT

Every up-to-date library and bookstore in this country has a shelf filled with nonfiction works of sexual advice, such as the previously mentioned *The Sensuous Man* and *The Sensuous Woman.* Among the most popular of these books are the works of Dr. Ruth Westheimer, an author who enjoys celebrity status. On a recent television broadcast, "Dr. Ruth" told a counselee, "Get this in your mind: in the imagination, nothing is forbidden."

In 1986, a group of upper-middle-class women in the San Francisco Bay area began meeting over luncheons of Brie and white wine to share sexual fantasies. They called themselves the "Ladies' Erotica Society," and went on to publish a book about their fantasies that, to the surprise of their publisher, sold 100,000 copies in three months. The stories varied widely—from one woman's fantasy about making love to the Pope to another's daydreams about seducing a teenage truck driver.

With the publication of *My Secret Garden* and *Forbidden Flowers,* popular author Nancy Friday has moved from books of research on interpersonal relationships to books that merely record female fantasies. Available in any bookstore to anyone, these two volumes are often as explicit as books in "adult" bookstores.

Outselling these nonfiction books by far are the fictional romances.

Fantasy tugs at our hearts from the pages of a new breed of romantic novels, which are being churned out by the millions. Just one publisher of pulp romance, Mills and Boon, has sold over 250 million romance novels. "Romance is big business," reports Merrill Congers, manager of a Los Angeles store in the B. Dalton chain. "I am aware of some customers who purchase two or three new titles a week."

In these books, the romantic male is mysterious, strong, usually but not always dark, sexually experienced, and described in implicitly sexual terms. A good example is Raoul in Mary Stewart's *Nine Coaches Waiting*. Raoul suffered emotionally but was not perverted beyond redemption; he had sexual experience, but Linda's innocence and love domesticate him with little struggle. These images may cause problems in the selection of a mate: They may set a young girl up for feeling, "I can change this man no matter what his problems have been."

As discussed in Kay Mussel's *Fantasy and Reconciliation,* mate selection has traditionally been a key theme in women's fiction:

Many women writers from the most serious to the most derivative, write within or against the fairy tale model, leaving unexamined the issues of a future *beyond* marriage. Nowhere in Jane Austen, with the possible exception of the Crofts in *Persuasion* and the Gardeners in *Pride and Prejudice,* do we find models for a marriage to which a woman might aspire (and the Crofts and Gardeners are minor characters).

At its best, the story can be rich and engaging in the hands of a Jane Austen or Charlotte Brontë or Mary Stewart; the story of a young girl's struggle toward adult identity has a resonance far beyond that of most popular romances. But the years of life after marriage were never covered. Only in the exquisite torture of mate selection and courtship do heroines in these stories appear to come alive, face real choices, and act fully as human characters with a meaningful role to play.

It was not until the mid—1970s, however, that romance novels routinely included total sexual encounters. Until then, romantic scenes were emotionally touching but not sexually explicit. Now, secular publishers' guidelines for would-be writers of romance indicate that heroines who go to bed with their lovers are the norm. The novels of Jackie Collins and Danielle Steel follow the lucrative "tell all" formula.

Barbara Cartland, the queen of Regency romances, objects to the increased portrayal of sexual acts in romantic novels: "Images of sex, especially sex by force, affect the brain, and this is the kind of sexuality that is pandered to by some of the new novels—some women's romances have become 'soft porn,' and this is a grave mistake."

The introduction of sex into romance novels has been paralleled by the growth of the so-called soft porn magazine industry. When *Playgirl* magazine was first issued, skeptics predicted that it would fold within months. "There is not a large enough audience among women for that sort of publication," they said. But *Playgirl* now claims a circulation of 10 million and has been joined by a host of other similar magazines.

These publications have had great impact on the "homemaker monthlies," which have begun to print stories that are "somewhat erotic." Women's journals such as *Cosmopolitan*, less coy than the homemaker monthlies, are now packed with articles of sexual advice and stories of sexual conquest.

An editor of a women's magazine writes, "A reader may not plan for a piece to affect her, but I know that the desire of every author is to affect the reader completely."

A woman whose letter was included in the March 1988 issue of *Family Circle* magazine wrote, "Every time I'd pick up a magazine or turn on the TV, I'd hear about all this mind-expanding sex people were having." This California wife and mother of two preschoolers explained her affair by saying, "I felt like I was the only person left who had had sex with one person. . . ."

FOR YOUR PERSONAL PLEASURE

In New York, San Francisco, Las Vegas, and other large cities, "fantasy theaters" are a growing trend. Theatergoers await their turn and, for an exorbitant amount, tell the actors their fantasy, which is then acted out on the stage. Fantasy in 3-D.

Another example of this new freedom on stage is the popular touring group of male strippers billed as Chippendales. Their show has moved out of nightclubs and discos and has now played to packed female audiences in opera houses and music halls across America.

In many local papers, individuals are invited to "have an affair by telephone. Sexy, interesting partners will share wild fantasies with you over the phone. Credit cards accepted." Of course.

We can never forget that the imagination is an important component of sexuality—but many individuals are choosing to *live* in fantasy.

Newsweek reporter David Ansen, compiling data on women's new freedom of fantasy, concluded his article with this thoughtful question: "All of this said—where does it leave modern men and women? In Liberation Land, U.S.A.? Or on separate but equal Fantasy Islands?"

THE FANTASY GAMES

For younger Americans, the glitter of the unreal leads from the big screen to video arcades and beyond. Junior high and high school students not only devour romantic and sexual fantasies, but also give a great deal of time and attention to science fiction and mystical, magical adventure. The most popular game-cult in America is the role-playing game "Dungeons & Dragons."

The players' handbook says, " 'Dungeons & Dragons' is a fantasy game of role-playing which relies upon the imagination of its participants, yet it is so mind-unleashing that it comes near reality. This is a game where monsters, good and evil priests, fierce demons, and even the gods themselves may enter your character's life."

In one recent year sales of "D & D" to young people were well over $260 million, and a computerized version is now used in hundreds of high schools across the nation to teach computing skills. Many adults have expressed great concern about the effects of "Dungeons & Dragons" on avid players. These concerns center on the amount of time it can take for one game to be completed; as a player identifies with his character over weeks and even months, incredible personality changes may occur. Indifference to real life, despair, and even clinical depression and some suicides have been attributed to long-term addiction to this "game." The concern is so far-reaching that the national PTA has expressed written opposition to the game.

Many adults do not realize that "Dungeons & Dragons" even includes a succubus. A succubus is a demon that can materialize in female form and have intercourse with a human male. The "D & D" manual says, "The kiss of a succubus drains the victim of his energy level, but is often addictive."

There are, of course, fantasy games and experiences for young people that are not nearly as questionable. Disney's technicians, for example, have developed "computer capsules" that add physical effects to scenes viewed on large computer screens. Disneyland's Star Tours ride, that utilizes the capsules, is only a prototype of what is planned for the future. "In these capsules," reports a technician, "we can make the participant experience the force of gravity as his spaceship blasts off, the feeling of freefall, and a myriad of other physical sensations which can almost turn fantasy into reality."

Isaac Asimov, one of the most prolific writers of science fiction, expresses concern about images we have absorbed through the technological marvels of modern entertainment. Asimov fears that too often young students entering the field of science feel that we are "far down the road" in space technology when in fact there is no such thing as, for example, "travel at warp speed." When confronted with the reality of where we are, young scientists sometimes grow impatient and quit. They are not willing to work through the nitty-gritty of making mankind's fondest dreams into reality.

It is so much easier to be entertained. After all, in the words of the Disney technician, we can "almost turn fantasy into reality."

It is exciting and exhilarating—and very, very addictive.

THE DILEMMA

What do you believe about the impact of fantasy on our modern culture? How do you feel about the impact of fantasy on your own life? On the lives of children coming to maturity during the fantasy deluge? Are the romantic expectations of this generation of women different from those of past generations?

Are our fantasies and mind trips "harmless, totally neutral and natural," as some psychologists report? Since the imagination is a part of our sexuality, is it true that "Fantasy Will Set You Free" as the book title suggests?

Are real-life relationships harmed by imaginary lovers? Even more personal is the question, *Why should I give up the perfection of my romantic fantasies for the imperfection of reality?*

THE SURVEY

In preparation for this book, a fantasy survey was mailed to 200,000 people across America in the May 1986 issue of *Virtue*, a West Coast-based women's magazine with subscribers of all ages and from all walks of life. The amazing responses (reported in the following two chapters), and the results of a national survey done at Columbia University have contributed greatly to our understanding of the romantic thought-life of twentieth-century American women.

Before continuing this book, it will be helpful if you answer for yourself the questions included in the survey.

FEMININE FANTASIES AND DAYDREAMS

What part do romantic daydreams and fantasies play in your life? Do they leave you unsatisfied with your marriage or spawn unrealistic expectations? More importantly, what part do day-dreams play in long-term emotional health and happiness? The following survey could be an eye-opener for you. (Disregard any questions that do not apply to your particular situation.)

1. Age: ——

2. Marital status:
   Married ——   Never married ——
   Divorced ——   Separated ——
   Widowed ——

3. When I daydream, my thoughts most often center on:
   _____ A. Dreams of fame or recognition for talents, abilities, or career.
   _____ B. Romance.
   _____ C. A different lifestyle (with fewer responsibilities, more money, or more adventure).

4. I find myself daydreaming or fantasizing:
   _____ A. Often.
   _____ B. Sometimes.
   _____ C. Hardly ever.

5. I believe my personal daydreams are the result of:
   _____ A. Boredom.
   _____ B. A troubled lifestyle from which escape is desirable.
   _____ C. Normal human creativity.

6. As a Christian, my attitude toward my own daydreams and fantasies is:
   _____ A. Usually comfortable.
   _____ B. Somewhat convicted.
   _____ C. Guilty or condemned.

7. My imagination is gripped by fearful thoughts such as a traffic accident or the loss of a loved one:
   _____ A. Almost daily.
   _____ B. Sometimes.
   _____ C. Seldom.

8. When involved in a romantic fantasy, my thoughts usually center on:
   _____ A. A famous person, such as an actor.
   _____ B. An imagined "Prince Charming."
   _____ C. My husband and I in another setting (such as a romantic cruise).

9. When making love with my husband, I fantasize:
   _____ A. Always.
   _____ B. Sometimes.
   _____ C. Seldom.

10. In these fantasies, I imagine that:
    _____ A. I am different.
    _____ B. My husband is different.
    _____ C. Our situation is different (for example, we are alone on a secluded island).

11. I feel comfortable sharing my daydreams and romantic longings with my husband.
    _____ A. Yes.
    _____ B. No.

12. I enjoy reading romantic novels such as gothic love stories:
    _____ A. Often.
    _____ B. Sometimes.
    _____ C. Seldom.

13. Because of my temperament and imagination, I feel it is most important to avoid television shows or other entertainment that breeds feelings of:
    _____ A. Fear.
    _____ B. Sorrow or despair.
    _____ C. Erotic longing.

14. I believe that the amount of time individuals spend daydreaming or in fantasy is increasing.
    _____ A. Yes.
    _____ B. No.

There are, of course, no right or wrong answers to these questions. Your honest answers will, however, help you to think deeply about your own thought-life. Perhaps some of your daydreams concern you. Perhaps others bring confusion and questions. Still other areas of your thought-life may have previously escaped consideration.

There are a great many wonderful uses for the imagination:

- Imagery can help us to reduce stress (including the stress that would keep us from sexual fulfillment).
- Daydreams can help us to plan our future.
- Imagery can help us to gain control over undesirable habits.
- The imagination of mankind enhances the real world through artistic expression and inventive genius.
- Our imaginings can help us learn about ourselves and our uniqueness.
- Our ability to daydream gives amusement in idle moments, allows us to relive pleasant moments of the past, and heightens our enjoyment of music, literature, and the arts.
- The imagination *is* an important component of feminine sexual fulfillment.

Dreams and Delusions is designed to help you examine your thoughts, your fantasies, your daydreams, and your images of romance. The imagination is not condemned, simply considered. We can be those who follow the eternal wisdom of the book of Proverbs:

"Consider your heart, its secret thoughts and feelings, with all vigilance . . . for out of this flow the springs of your life" (Prov. 4:3).

Chapter Two

The Days of Our Lives

T HE most comforting words that can ever be spoken to a human being are the words "YOU ARE NOT ALONE."

It is important to know that we are not alone in the feelings that we have or in our thoughts. It is important to know that we are not the first to have faced whatever struggle we are facing—to know that we are not the only one who has ever confronted a certain question, temptation, or dilemma.

Women from all fifty states responded to the fantasies and daydreams survey. They ranged in age from seventeen to seventy-two years old (the majority were between twenty-three and fifty-five). Seventeen percent had not married, 66 percent were married, 15 percent were separated or divorced, and 2 percent were widows. Some 9,500 surveys were returned in time to be compiled in these statistics. Many were unsigned, but other women included their names and addresses.

A most astonishing result of the survey was that over 800 questionnaires were returned with letters, many of which gave lengthy personal histories. *"I just have to write,"* commented one woman, *"because someone has finally asked the questions for which **many** of us need answers."*

The women who included letters all expressed an eagerness to talk openly and honestly about fantasies and daydreams, though their issues varied. Some shared humorous anecdotes; others heartbreaking realities, great confusion, and a deep conviction that something was wrong. Some letters came from women who have found inner happiness as they were able to integrate the different components of feminine sexuality. Other women wrote from a dungeon of despair.

The survey results are given below. Many comments from the letters are also included in this chapter and throughout the book.

FEMININE FANTASIES AND DAYDREAMS

Survey Results

1. Age: 17–72

2. Marital status:

Married	66%	Never married	17%
Divorced	11%	Separated	4%
Widowed	2%		

3. When I daydream, my thoughts most often center on:

   28% A. Dreams of fame or recognition for talents, abilities, or career.

   40% B. Romance.

   32% C. A different lifestyle (with fewer responsibilities, more money, or more adventure).

4. I find myself daydreaming or fantasizing:

   25% A. Often.

   59% B. Sometimes.

   16% C. Hardly ever.

5. I believe my personal daydreams are the result of:

    29% A. Boredom.

    23% B. A troubled lifestyle from which escape is desirable.

    48% C. Normal human creativity.

6. As a Christian, my attitude toward my own daydreams and fantasies is:

    35% A. Usually comfortable.

    39% B. Somewhat convicted.

    26% C. Guilty or condemned.

7. My imagination is gripped by fearful thoughts such as a traffic accident or the loss of a loved one:

    21% A. Almost daily.

    46% B. Sometimes.

    33% C. Seldom.

8. When involved in a romantic fantasy, my thoughts usually center on:

    17% A. A real person, such as an actor.

    40% B. An imagined "Prince Charming."

    43% C. My husband and I in another setting (such as a romantic cruise).

9. When making love with my husband, I fantasize:

    24% A. Always.

    42% B. Sometimes.

    34% C. Seldom.

10. In these fantasies, I imagine that:

    30% A. I am different.

    21% B. My husband is different.

    49% C. Our situation is different (for example, we are alone on a secluded island).

11. I feel comfortable sharing my daydreams and romantic longings with my husband.
    <u>47.5%</u> A. Yes.
    <u>52.5%</u> B. No.

12. I enjoy reading romantic novels such as gothic love stories:
    <u>20%</u> A. Often.
    <u>45%</u> B. Sometimes.
    <u>35%</u> C. Seldom.

13. Because of my temperament and imagination, I feel it is most important to avoid television shows or other entertainment that breeds feelings of:
    <u>37%</u> A. Fear.
    <u>24%</u> B. Sorrow or despair.
    <u>39%</u> C. Erotic longing.

14. I believe that the amount of time individuals spend daydreaming or in fantasy is increasing.
    <u>63%</u> A. Yes.
    <u>37%</u> B. No.

OF CYCLES AND SEASONS: AN OVERVIEW

The survey illustrated that there are cycles and seasons in our lives, for the answers to some of the questions were affected by a woman's age.

For example, 40 percent of the women who responded to question #3 said that their daydreams most often revolve around romance. Of these women, a full 72 percent were in their late twenties or thirties. This is the stage of life when a woman's sexual drive reaches its peak. It is also the stage when many women have been married for a few years and find their husbands deeply involved in careers and their own lives filled with the demanding routine of child rearing.

Of the women who answered question #3 by saying that they most often daydream about recognition or a different lifestyle, 60 percent were in their forties. This seems to be a season of life when many women long not just for romance, but for greater meaning and fulfillment than they have achieved. It is a time when many women sense that adjustments must be made and that new goals are needed.

Responses to question #7 were also affected by the age of the women. The 21 percent who reported being gripped by fearful fantasies were usually either women in their late twenties and early thirties (young marrieds caring for small children) or women in their late forties and their fifties (women who are often dealing with physical and hormonal changes).

How our age and season affects our thought-life will be considered in later chapters. Of course, many women's responses did not "fit" the basic patterns. A college professor from Iowa wrote: "I am 48 years old with grown children, a good husband, and a fulfilling career—but I have never dealt with romantic and sexual fantasies like I do now. I can't help but believe that I am being affected by the changing attitudes of our society. I have a happy life, but somehow my *appetite for romance* just keeps growing."

Notice that although this woman's feelings do not fit the basic pattern, they fit with the fact that 63 percent of those polled say they believe the amount of time individuals spend daydreaming or in fantasy *is* increasing.

One social worker wrote: "It seems to me that we are in a season in our society when it is pretty easy to choose *not* to live in reality; we have so many forms of entertainment, so many diversions. As I get to know the young women I am assigned to counsel, I am amazed at how many of them spend a great deal of time daydreaming. Besides all of the media input which triggers daydreaming, I think a lot of people give in to spending a lot of time in fantasy because of an overall feeling of *hopelessness about reality*."

ARE YOU COMFORTABLE WITH YOUR FANTASIES?

One in four women find themselves daydreaming often, and only 16 percent said that they seldom fantasize or daydream (question #4). Yet of all of those who returned the questionnaire, only 35 percent report that they are comfortable with the themes of their fantasies (question #6). Thirty-nine percent reported feeling somewhat convicted about their fantasies, while 26 percent felt outright guilt or condemnation.

Here are comments from three women's letters:

"I have never been able to understand just *why* I have some of the sexual fantasies that I do. They certainly are not things that my husband would suspect that I think about. I have always wondered just why certain ideas seem to 'turn me on.' "

"The woman I am in my fantasies and the woman I am in real life are two different people. To enter into a relationship with a man that I may daydream about would be too destructive to my children and husband. And of course it would hurt my husband terribly if he knew I daydreamed about one of his close friends."

"My feelings of guilt have come because I let my fantasies begin to center on someone other than my husband, and he is a man who would not even be a good husband. In my heart I was being unfaithful. For a while I was so convicted that I thought my head would burst, literally, from the pressure. It is taking real willpower to turn away. I have run to the Bible and to prayer for strength, and I am finding that God wants to help me."

For some women, the time spent on fantasizing was itself a problem. Here are the comments of two women who said they fantasize often:

"In the past few years I have been struggling with this problem of daydreaming. It came to the point that I resented my husband and household duties because they interrupted my daydream escapes! I looked for excuses to spend time alone. I truly began to be cut off from reality."

"I had always planned to do so much when my children started school, but now I find that I waste so much time! I know that my mental attitude will improve if I can discipline myself to action."

WHERE IS YOUR FOCUS?

In response to the question about the focus of romantic fantasies (question #8), 43 percent said that they focus on their husbands in another setting. The following two comments were typical:

"Let's face it, sex is fulfilling, but it can become so routine. I believe that fantasizing about your husband (such as being on a beach in Hawaii) is all right. It helps me to forget all the little pressures of daily life."

"I find that romantic 'getaways' with my husband, from a weekend at a nearby motel to a candlelight dinner out, come to my mind later and bring excitement and satisfaction."

Forty percent of those responding to question #8, however, tend to focus on an imagined "Prince Charming." Another 17 percent admit fantasizing about a real person other than their mate—whether a co-worker, a close friend or distant acquaintance, or even a former boyfriend.

One woman wrote, "My romantic fantasies make me wonder if I ever really got over my old boyfriend, yet if he were here in reality, I doubt that I would choose him over my husband."

Another said, "I was being really troubled by romantic fantasies about a man I work with. The daydreams went on for quite a while, and finally, I shared my thoughts with a close girlfriend. Somehow, just getting these fantasies out into the light has made them loose their hold on me. But I know that it is only smart to share your deepest inner thoughts with someone you can really trust."

Women who fantasize about a man they know offered insight into the dangers involved. For example, Brenda wrote: "Sometimes men I meet at work may appear to be more of a Prince Charming than my husband. I do not imagine actual sexual encounters, but I imagine them noticing me and complimenting me. Even though these thoughts may not seem evil, I know they could lead to trouble. It is so tempting to flirt, to play the old game 'just to see' if I can get the man to be attracted to me."

Although women may daydream of other men, it is not their husbands that most women seek to change. As responses to question #10 show, the women who dream of a different situation wish to change themselves (30 percent) more than they wish to change their spouses (21 percent)!

The women who fantasized about "a new self" often focused on physical characteristics. Here are the comments of three women who had such fantasies:

"If I don't *feel* attractive, I can't enjoy my husband's advances. I usually imagine that I am the thin, tanned, lovely woman that I want to be. I suppose I should stop imagining that and work toward that goal in real life."

"Yes, I imagine that I am different, sometimes with long black hair, sometimes with blond hair and blue eyes. I look okay, but I guess I want to feel more beautiful and desirable, and I don't think these fantasies are wrong. They add so much to my feelings of sexuality."

"I was in an auto accident that left some pretty bad scars on my body. I used to imagine that they were all gone, until my husband told me that he never had to imagine the scars away! Now I feel comfortable with myself, just the way I am."

Of the women who fantasized their husband was different, most wanted their mates to be *more expressive*. Here is what two women had to say:

"If only my husband could remember how important words are to me! I dream of him saying things that he would never say in real life. He is a real silent type."

"Ever since I was a little girl, I have devoured romantic novels. I do wish American men were *taught* to be more expressive and romantic. . . . I don't think my expectations are too great."

ROMANCE

Forty percent of those surveyed said they most often daydream about romance. The following comment was typical: "I have three little ones, and I often daydream about 'the Good Old Days' when I was popular at college and received much masculine attention. I guess I feel that my dating days were the highlight of my life. Why am I not more satisfied with the season of life I am in now?"

SHARING WITH SPOUSE

There were mixed responses to the question about sharing fantasies with the spouse (question #11). The women were closely divided between those who felt comfortable sharing fantasies (47.5 percent), and those who did not (52.5 percent).

Some women suggested this communication was a positive one. "At first, I guess I thought my husband would laugh at me if I told him the compliments I imagined he was giving me. But when I finally shared, he started learning to be more expressive. He also felt able to tell me about his longings for me to be more free and less inhibited. Our ability to talk has helped us greatly."

But others warned of dangers. "My husband and I were sharing our fantasies, but in a *wrong* way. Before, we used fantasy and pornography as stimulants. But we have felt we should turn away from this. We came to this decision together, and we have discovered a more beautiful sexual relationship because of it."

FANTASIES DURING LOVEMAKING

Although 34 percent of those surveyed said that they seldom fantasize during lovemaking, 42 percent said that they sometimes fantasize and 24 percent that they always fantasize (question #9). Feelings about such fantasies were mixed.

Judy wrote, "I often daydream about when my husband and I met. It was wartime, and he was a soldier who swept me off my feet. To other people he may be overweight and aging, but to me he is still that handsome young officer that I love."

But two other women were troubled by their fantasies: "What an area of struggle for me! I almost always fantasize when making love to my husband, and I seem unable to become excited without fantasizing. To me, thoughts of romantic conquest are what bring excitement. My husband is tender and gentle, but many times I am not really 'here' when we are making love, and he must sense that."

"I am very unhappy about this area of my life. I used to fantasize romantically during sex to have orgasms, but I heard from some people that *all* fantasy is wrong. I have stopped using my imagination at all, and I feel that my husband and I have suffered because of it. I have very sincere questions that still need answers."

DREAMS OF A DIFFERENT LIFESTYLE

Of those surveyed, 32 percent reported they most often daydream about a different lifestyle. Three women explain the function these daydreams serve.

"It is extremely hard for me to enjoy intimacy unless I picture myself with my husband away from the children. It must be the price for living in a very small house!"

"I had a real problem with fantasies and daydreams for thirteen years of my seventeen-year marriage. I dreamed of a more comfortable lifestyle with more money and nicer clothes. These daydreams often included more recognition and romance. Let's face it—little children seldom compliment their mothers, and husbands often forget."

"A lot of the tasks we moms perform are pretty mundane, and so when I'm sweeping or mopping, I imagine that I'm a hero in the Peace Corps, or taking part in an expedition, or doing a lot of other things that my kids would find really very humorous."

FEARFUL IMAGININGS

Questions #7 and #13 dealt not with romantic fantasies, but with fears and other promptings of the imagination. Two-thirds of the women surveyed admitted to more than occasional fears, including 21 percent who said that they almost daily worry needlessly about personal tragedy.

A woman from Maryland commented that she had lived in constant fear that something would happen to her first baby.

Learning to control her fearful imagination brought new peace. Only then did motherhood become "a wonderful exercise in learning to trust Jesus one day at a time."

Another woman commented, "I am one of those women who really has to avoid movies or TV shows or books that would cause fearful pictures to stay in my mind. Why do some of us struggle with fear so often? I want to learn the balance between being careful with my children (and teaching them to be careful) and being a 'smothering' mother who causes her kids to be filled with fear."

A woman from Chicago noted that she often had sorrowful daydreams in which she became the object of greater concern to her family (having a critical illness, e.g.). She once thought these dreams were rooted in childhood fears but on reflection came to recognize that they were the result of self-pity. Another woman, however, did see her fears as the direct result of a difficult childhood. As she experiences the healing of new-found faith, she anticipates that she will no longer be tormented by such thoughts and dreams.

ROMANTIC NOVELS

For some women, romantic novels appear to be a positive outlet. "I choose to read because the kind of stories I choose are so much more wholesome than the kind of stories that are on television."

For others, they are unimportant. "Actually, I have very little time for reading because of the age of my children. When I do have a chance to read, I usually choose nonfiction, such as articles about family living!"

For a third group of women, romance novels are a serious stumbling block. "For me, reading romance is wrong because I tend to be *overly* sentimental, and even good love stories make me restless and somewhat dissatisfied with my own life."

MEDIA INFLUENCE

Some women feel they are *not* much influenced by the media.
Jan wrote to say that she does not think that her viewing affects
her thought-life. "When I come home after a long day at the
office, I want *entertainment*. Of course I am not silly enough
to believe that every time Jessica Fletcher [in "Murder, She
Wrote"] visits an old friend a murder happens right before
her eyes, or that there could possibly be as many gorgeous
guys and gals in one spot as there are in just one episode of a
miniseries. I just tell myself afterwards 'That isn't reality.' Any
sane adult can keep reality separated from fantasy."

Similarly, Yolanda says, "I have learned just to *talk back* to
my television. If a commercial insults my intelligence, I just
tell it so! But I am glad that the stars on the tube don't look
the way my husband and I look in the morning. If they did,
I wouldn't watch them!"

The majority of women, however, reported that they sometimes have problems with fantasies and that the media are
often involved. Darlene, for example, wrote. "Our imaginations are so stirred these days with all of the media and advertising. I don't think other generations had to deal with all
of the input that we deal with today.

"I have inner battles in my mind. This is what the Bible
calls 'spiritual warfare,' isn't it? My spiritual self rages against
my old self."

One woman commented on the need for discernment and
"self-censorship" in both television viewing and music listening. Country music songs, she noted, often promote infidelity
more than rock songs!

Others expressed shock and disbelief at the content of current
television shows, especially noting violence. Said one woman,
"I avoid them, and I make certain my children avoid them.
If I watched these programs, I feel certain that I would be

afraid to drive down the street, to walk to the drugstore or even to leave my home!"

According to the comments, television often leads its viewers to feel fear, sadness, and erotic longings. "Certain scenes flash back into my mind again and again," noted one respondent. "Whatever I feed into my imagination stays in my mental computer for a long time."

OTHER CAUSES

Aside from the media, a variety of causes stimulated troubling fantasies and daydreaming. The following three women each addressed a different cause:

"I find that I daydream more when I have been stuck in the house for more than a few days because of bad weather, a child's illness, etc. I have found that isolation is an enemy."

"My husband and I have had an emotional divorce for a long time. He is very cold, and romantic fantasy fills a void in my life. It helps to make life with my husband bearable. I know I need to seek help."

"There is so much talk today about women 'finding themselves' that I am afraid it is making my two married daughters very restless."

POSITIVE CHANNELS

Proper use of the imagination is crucial. One woman wrote, "God gave us a wonderful gift when He gave us our imaginations, didn't He? The trick is to channel our imaginations into things that are constructive rather than things that are destructive. I am a sexual being, and I will always have some romantic and sexual longings, but I need God's wisdom so that they don't run wild and become destructive."

(36)

Many women spoke specifically of spiritual use of the imagination. "I love to read books like *The Chronicles of Narnia*; they help my mind expand in its understanding of what heaven will be."

"Since we visited Israel, I always try to picture the Bible verses that I am reading. This has helped me a great deal in applying the Bible to my daily life."

"I have not used my imagination in the right way in the past. I have not really stopped to realize that there could be wonderful spiritual uses for my imagination. But this week I am going to try the formula found in Philippians, chapter 4. I'm going to think about things that are lovely, things that deserve praise, things of 'good report.'"

Another woman shared a different perspective on the dangers of an overactive imagination: "I was involved in Eastern thought before I became a true Christian. I was taught to use my mind in things such as soul travel. I have wanted to be very careful with my imagination because I don't want to get back into deception."

A PLEA FOR HELP

Many letters were unsigned, and other writers asked that their names be kept confidential, but in her plea for help Devi Mitchell made no such request. "I am not afraid to admit that I have a lot of nitty-gritty questions and haven't known where to turn for answers," Devi wrote. "I grew up without a mother or sisters, and I have never heard our pastor or other speakers deal with this complicated issue of feminine sexuality.

"I lost my mother to mental illness, so believe me, I know firsthand the power of fantasies and delusions. . . .

"My mind is a cluttered mess. I was raised without much discipline, and now when I want to discipline my thoughts, I don't even know where to begin. I feel so out of control. I guess I expected that when we 'Cinderellas' grew up, life in the castle would be easier."

SUMMER O'BRIAN: ONE WOMAN'S STORY IN DEPTH

This is the life story of a young woman whose disappointments with reality led her to cling to daydreams and delusions.

Summer first dreamed of him when she was only fourteen years old. . . .

In the dream she was standing on a familiar pier, gazing into the turquoise water of Morro Bay. Suddenly a sailing sloop appeared directly in front of her. A young man stood and held out his hand. He was tall and tanned. His slenderness accented high cheekbones and a masculine jawline. His hair was black and wavy, but its glory was overshadowed by the piercing blue of his eyes.

Summer grasped the hand he extended and stepped into the boat. With his strong arm around her, she and the stranger sailed away. . . .

That was all there was to the dream. But when she awoke, her heart was pounding. The dream had seemed so real. She dressed quickly and walked to school.

All through that day, through her classes and even through the quiet supper she shared with Mamma, Summer felt that she was surrounded by a hazy mist. The simple dream, and the striking man in that dream, was so vivid in her mind that it made the real world seem like a fantasy.

She didn't tell anyone at the time. Summer O'Brian, even at fourteen, was a very private girl.

She was also a very pretty girl. Her thick blond mane hung long and perfectly straight in an era when some of her girlfriends were actually ironing theirs to achieve the straight look. Her features were finely chiseled. She thought of her figure as medium and her height as medium and her eyes as "a medium sort of gray." In reality, those gray eyes were large and wide set and were complemented by full, expressive lips.

Throughout junior high and high school, Summer's beauty brought her a series of admirers. She could have dated more if she had not been so shy, so painfully shy. To many young men, her reserve made her seem almost unapproachable.

Sometimes Summer developed a mad crush on an admirer. Sometimes she would even dream of him. Usually she grew tired of a boyfriend before he tired of her. Then she would remember the perfect looks of the dream stranger in the sailboat and think about him. Some nights she would dream again of the stranger; he would play the role of a date for a prom, or a football hero, or even a prince.

During her teen years Summer was often alone. She had no brothers or sisters, and her father had died when she was nine years old. He had drowned in a scuba diving accident off the California coast. The O'Brian household contained just Summer and Mamma, and Mamma had to work long hours at a grocery store to make ends meet.

When Summer graduated from Morro Bay High School in 1969, she hated to leave her mother home alone. But she had worked her way to a scholarship at Stanford University. It was a prestigious open door, so Summer summoned all her courage and walked through it.

Stanford was a wonderful new world. At first Summer didn't think she was going to make it, scholastically or emotionally. She settled herself into the dormitory and studied as hard as any student on campus.

College life was so hectic that Summer was sometimes actually physically dizzy. Shyness fell away because she didn't have the *time* to be shy. Lectures were interesting and she found herself entering class discussions before she had time to think. Because the young men on campus were interested in the same subjects that she was, Summer was even able to relax and communicate when she went on a date. She no longer dreamed about the stranger.

Summer met Daniel in October of her sophomore year. They bumped into each other—literally—at a campus peace rally. Daniel's husky body knocked her fragile one to the concrete. "I beg your pardon, fair maiden," he grinned, easily lifting Summer to her feet. "The least I can do for a poor damsel in distress is to offer her some cool refreshment." And he had taken her arm and guided her to a Coke stand before she could even protest.

Daniel Page was a native New Yorker. Sandy hair and a boyish grin, an Eastern accent and the confident walk of a healthy young athlete somehow combined to remind Summer of the Kennedy clan. The only hint that Daniel was a serious student of law was that he wore scholarly wire-rimmed glasses.

Summer had never known anyone who was as much fun to be with as Daniel Page. His quick wit kept her laughing. His keen mind kept her thinking. Their dates were times of doing everything from marching in demonstrations to walking through museums to swinging in a playground like small children. Before the semester ended, Summer moved out of the dorm and into Daniel's studio apartment.

That summer, Summer found that she was pregnant. She was afraid to tell Daniel, but when she did he just laughed. They were married in August, and little Angela Page arrived on Christmas Eve.

For a while Summer was happy, extremely happy. She loved being a mother, even though it meant leaving college. She loved being a wife . . . that is, when she had a chance to be a wife. Between Daniel's classes and his heavy load of homework and the job he had gotten to supplement his student loan, his time with Summer was almost nonexistent. And Summer discovered that when Daniel was under pressure, his happy-go-lucky personality gave way to depression and fits of anger.

When Angela was six months old, Summer got a job as a newspaper reporter. "The extra money will relieve Daniel's pressure," she thought. "Besides, since he's too busy for me, I have to fill my life with something more."

The job did not solve the problems of the turbulent highs and lows of her husband's personality. Loud arguments became a daily fact of life. By the time Angela was a year old, Summer asked Daniel for a divorce. "The marriage was a mistake," she told herself. "Daniel was just not the right kind of man for me."

Todd was different. . . .

He came to work at the newspaper soon after Summer's divorce was final. Todd was not a college man; he was a poor boy from the South who was working his way up the ladder with grit and determination. Daniel had been blond and well-mannered and sensitive. Todd was dark-complected, rough as a cowboy, strong-minded, and manly. He was a little bit like the black-haired stranger she had first dreamed of as a girl. She was more physically attracted to Todd Colten than to any man she had ever met.

Todd and Summer were married in 1973. He already owned a home, and as he moved Summer and Angela into the cozy bungalow, Mrs. Colten thought she had found a man she could depend on, a man who would make her secure.

Over the next few years, Summer discovered that she could *not* depend on Todd. She could not depend on him to stay sober. The strong temperament she had thought so manly and appealing could become violent when he had been drinking. She could not depend on Todd to keep away from drugs. She could not depend on his faithfulness.

One night in September 1976, Todd stumbled into the house in a drunken rage. He slapped four-year-old Angela, sending her reeling against the wall. He grabbed a butcher knife from the kitchen and turned on his wife. Summer lifted her whimpering daughter and ran to safety at a neighbor's.

She never went back.

After the second divorce was final, Summer was hurt and confused and bitter. She decided that she and Angela would be far better off without a man in their lives. She quit her job, and moved home to Morro Bay so that Angela could be near Grandma and in the peace of a small town.

Summer rarely dated. Instead, for the first time in years, she had dreams about the stranger.

Youthful romantic fantasies had been put aside in the busyness of college days and the career that followed. Now, whenever there was a moment to spare, Summer devoured novels by authors like Janet Dailey. It was easy to justify the amount of time she spent daydreaming about imaginary lovers—the real men she had cared for had brought bitter disappointment.

Summer accepted a job as the public relations director for a community hospital. There, she came in contact with William Harvey, a doctor.

Bill was thirty-seven, a full ten years older than Summer. He had been a widower for four years, having lost his wife in a tragic car accident. He and Summer became wonderful friends.

Dr. Harvey was one of the few churchgoing men that she had ever known. She teased him about it, and he responded by grinning and asking her to join him. For several weeks, she and Angela sat beside him in the worship services of New Hope Chapel. Summer loved the services; she had not been in church since grade school.

Then Summer began to sense that Bill was beginning to care for her, to think of her as much more than a friend. At first she felt a glimmer of hope in her heart. "He does not look exactly like a Prince Charming," she thought, smiling to herself. "I never picture Prince Charming losing his hair." But the warmth of his personality was incredibly attractive.

Bill seemed like such a wonderful man. Still, fear superseded the hope. Summer had been horribly wrong twice before. She did not want to be broken again.

Besides, something else was bothering her—the dreams about the stranger.

Suppose she was clairvoyant? Suppose there *was* a real man, somewhere, who embodied the man of her dreams? Odder things had happened. Summer had always been somewhat mystical, somewhat convinced that there was more to life than just physical realities.

What if the dream had come to her, through the years, to tell her who the real Mr. Right was? What if her marriages had gone bad because she had not waited for the one that fate had destined to be Mr. Right?

How could she know? How could she find out? And if the stranger of the dreams was not a representative of the "perfect man" who was out there somewhere, *wasn't it better to cling to the perfection of the imaginary than to be set up for the disappointments of reality?*

The more Bill Harvey began to care for her, the more troubled she became. For the first time in her life, Summer felt as if she were going crazy. For the first time in her life, she knew that she had to get help.

Good counselors are hard to find. Summer had talked to many outpatients at the hospital's mental health unit and had come to believe that even credentialed psychologists could be confusing and unhelpful. She determined that she would choose her counselor only by personal recommendations.

A nurse named Sally Lang gave Summer the name of a counselor at the family health clinic nearby. "I'm going to see her in two weeks myself," Sally reported. "I've heard from many sources that she's the best in the area."

Summer knew that Sally, too, was troubled by dreams, fearful dreams. "I'm haunted by fears that I can't seem to iron out on my own," Sally confided. Sally also admitted that, though she was happily married and the mother of two boys, she often was preoccupied with romantic fantasies about men other than her husband.

"Maybe," Sally said, "the counselor will have some answers for us both!"

Summer made an appointment and waited anxiously for the day to arrive. On a warm April morning in 1978, she drove to the address of the counselor's office. To her amazement, the family health clinic was located in an ivy-covered brick building just around the corner from Bill's church. The church and the office building had the same architectural style and seemed to be related.

Summer hesitated for a moment before she got out of her car. The brick building looked like an old fortress, and the ivy clinging to it made Summer think that its occupants might be like nuns or monks cloistered far from the real world. If the woman she was to see was some sort of church counselor, she might not relate to the hurts and questions in Summer's life. Still, the recent visits to the church had convinced Summer that the Bible *did* have wisdom for modern life.

"Besides, I've got an appointment," she told herself, and she headed up the steps of the counseling center. "And what have I got to lose? Maybe the doctor can tell me *something* about my dreams . . . and about why they are beginning to hold me back from real life."

Unraveling the Dream

During that first session at the family health clinic, Summer was amazed at the insight she gained from sharing with a trained professional her preoccupation with "the stranger."

The counselor pointed out that the original dream, in which Summer stood gazing into the water of the Pacific Ocean, could easily have been triggered by a subconscious longing for her father, who had been lost in that water. She gently told

Summer that it is normal for a young girl, especially one without a father, to long for a strong "Prince Charming" but that to allow an adolescent dream to shape her adult life was dangerous. The counselor ended their time together with a powerful statement: *"No flesh-and-blood man can ever live up to your fantasy."*

That first session was tear filled, and many more emotional sessions followed. Gradually, Summer began to understand the word "delusions," which psychologists define as "false beliefs that begin to affect our perception of ourselves and the world around us."

The counselor eventually asked Summer to look up several biblical references which dealt with "living in the Truth." Summer also discovered a New Testament statement of Jesus that says that mankind has a spiritual enemy and that this enemy is best described as "the Father of Lies," the author of delusions (chapter 8 of John).

Summer had always believed in the reality of the spiritual world, but she had never understood that it could have such impact on her daily life. She had never before discovered verses from Scripture that applied to her own situation.

Eight weeks had passed. Now, as Summer drove up to the family health clinic, the ivy-covered building looked like an old friend. Summer no longer thought of it as a cloistered hiding place from the world.

As the weeks had gone by, Summer had seen for the first time how some mistakes in her own way of thinking had contributed to the failure of both her marriages. She had come to realize that her counselor was right. No real man could ever measure up to a fantasy.

But even if that were true, the fantasy was still alluring compared to Todd and Daniel and all the other men she had known. After all, like the song said, "Imaginary lovers will never let you down, imaginary lovers are always around. . . ."

Summer was ready to admit that her dreams about the

stranger had not been "mystical," that she would not meet the stranger in the real world. But, after all, Summer thought, "it's not as if I fantasize all the time. I hold a good job; I function well on a daily basis." Why couldn't she have this new relationship with Bill and continue her daydream patterns?

She summarized her feelings in an honest, searching question for the counselor: *"Why should I choose imperfect reality over the glistening perfection of my fantasies?"*

Together, Summer and the counselor began the extensive search for the answer to that question, and this search became the basis for the material covered in this book.

AN EPIDEMIC?

Lee Ezell, motivational speaker and author of *The Missing Piece,* included this personal note with her survey response: "I am eager to read about the response to this survey, because as I speak across America, I am discovering a problem of epidemic proportions. It is an *epidemic of Cinderellas*! And Christian women are anything but vaccinated. As a matter of fact, some of us are the worst offenders, because we spiritualize the fairy tale."

In the early days of the Christian church, the Apostle Peter wrote an encouraging letter to a group of believers and said, "Remember, there has come upon you no strange affliction different from that which we all are facing at this time in history." (II Peter 5:9) In other words, "YOU ARE NOT ALONE."

There are a great many women who have questions, and who are disillusioned with the romance they find in reality because our only idea of what it means to be a "princess" or a "queen" comes from the ethereal world of fairy tales and the great American fantasy machine. We fall victims to the epidemic of Cinderellas until we realize that God offers us rulership in reality in a present-day kingdom (Rom. 5:17). The "Cinderella syndrome" may be simply our longing to find greater fulfillment and rulership, to be women whose lives are not "out of control."

That rulership in life begins as we come to a greater understanding of our femininity and sexuality . . .

as we come to understand our sexual fantasies (which will be discussed in Chapter 3) . . .

as we look beyond our fantasy longings to discover underlying needs (Chapter 4) . . .

and as we come to a greater appreciation of the treasure of the imagination.

Chapter Three

On Common Ground

"Oh God, you have made me amazingly complex."
Psalms 139:13

EACH of us has romantic and sexual fantasies. These imaginings are common to men and women, to people of every nationality and ethnicity, to generation after generation. In fact, romantic or sexual fantasizing is a step of human emotional development, as well as an expression of our very nature as sexual beings.

Most of us agree with the feelings of the woman who says: "I have never been able to understand just *why* I have some of the sexual fantasies that I do." In a young child, romantic imaginings may begin as early as four or five. A little girl may see the movie *Snow White* and begin to dream of a Prince Charming who will carry her away to his happy kingdom on a beautiful white horse. A little boy may imagine that he will grow up and marry his mother.

In her widely influential book *Your Child's Self-Esteem*, Dorothy Briggs points out that romantic images often begin with attachment to the parent of the opposite sex, usually occurring between the ages of three and five. She talks about the importance of parents' handling of such attachments:

(48)

Emotional attachment at this age provides a child with his first safe attempt at understanding a romantic relationship. If handled wisely, this attachment acts as an embryotic experience upon which the child will build in adolescence. Unless parents are aware of this stage, they may worry needlessly.

But, for example, when five-year-old Vera announced in front of both of her parents that she loved her daddy best and wanted to grow up to marry him, her mother reacted with wisdom.

"Yes, Vera," her mother replied. "You know most five-year-old little girls like their daddy best!"

This response let Vera know her feelings were acceptable. She was not shamed, nor did she lose approval.

Many adults have fantasies that are lengthy and elaborately developed. Other adults, and most children, have only fleeting, sketchy mental images.

Some childhood fantasies are based around mistaken notions that later become a part of the sexual arousal pattern for an individual. For example, a youngster who accidentally sees her parents making love may believe that they are fighting. Somehow fighting and sex may become woven together in her memory so that years later her fantasies of sexual encounters include physical roughness. However, confused fantasies are usually greatly altered by maturing sexual understanding.

As children grow older, their basic fantasy is elaborated by ideas from movies, books, and television. According to Dr. Eugene L. Goldberg, clinical professor of psychology at Albert Einstein College of Medicine, "adolescence is one long rehearsal fantasy." For example, romantic sexual fantasies help girls rehearse the responses to courtship they will make as young women. A fantasy may revolve around a favorite movie star, sparked by a poster of him. Especially during the junior high school years, hero worship with accompanying fantasies can fill a great portion of one's mental computer.

In adult life, fantasies serve many psychological purposes. The most common and important is that of arousing and maintaining sexual excitement. In the survey taken for this book, a surprising 66 percent of the women reported that they sometimes or always fantasize while making love.

Fantasies can enable us to shut out our surroundings while we concentrate on sensual feelings. A young mother with three children under five years of age confides her most common fantasy: "When my husband and I make love, I always imagine that we are alone on a beach of a Caribbean island. I imagine a warm starlit evening, the gentle ocean waves, the quiet tropical landscape. I love my children dearly, but somehow I am much more romantic if I forget about the piles of unfolded laundry, the unwashed dishes, the little cherubs sleeping downstairs!"

Other women may feel more sensual through fantasies in which they idealize their own physical appearance. "I do not feel guilty," one woman reports, "when I imagine myself in the beautifully tanned, twenty-five-pound lighter body that I had on our honeymoon. I find that when I feel unattractive, I cannot respond to my husband."

Dr. Alexander N. Levay, clinical professor of psychiatry at Columbia University College of Physicians and Surgeons in New York, gives the opinion of most doctors and counselors: "Sexual fantasies are a normal part of human behavior. But we are only beginning to discover what a wide variety of erotic fantasies people have. The uniqueness of one's sexual fantasies makes them dynamite. Are they harmless, private movies we can run for our own enjoyment? I think rather that they are *clues to our deepest desires or needs, fingerprints of the subconscious.*"

FOUR COMMON THEMES

Most psychologists begin by dividing sexual fantasies into two large categories: (1) fantasies that involve submission to someone else (e.g., because of feelings of overwhelming passion) and (2) fantasies of overpowering another and of conquest through sex appeal, charm, and so forth. Fantasies range from joyful surrender through mild aggression to extreme dominance.

Men most often have fantasies that are aggressive and women most often fantasies that are submissive, but it is not uncommon at times for fantasies to reverse these roles. Martha Gunzberg, director of a couples counseling center in New York City, says, "We all have many kinds of feelings inside us. In our minds we are master and slave, parent and child, seeker and one sought after."

Within the two large categories there are common themes. Each individual usually has one theme (with variations) which he or she calls on throughout life.

Researchers at Columbia University have collected hundreds of written sexual fantasies from women of all ages and all walks of life. Though each fantasy is unique, they do fall into four categories based on the themes they express.

By far the most common are fantasies of *pure romance*. Responses to the fantasy survey discussed in Chapter 2 included many examples of pure romance fantasies:

"I imagine that we are in another time period, another nation. . . ."

"I picture my husband as the strong, handsome young soldier he was when we met in England. . . ."

"It may sound corny, but I still imagine that I am a lady held captive, who is rescued by a brave knight. . . ."

A common fantasy that is a variation on the romance theme is that of romance with a famous person. "This is very common because you see celebrities every day on television and in magazines," says Dr. Levay. "You almost feel you know them. A woman knows it is much safer to fantasize about a famous figure than to have dreams about a forbidden figure, for example, a co-worker."

Younger women, especially teenagers, and women over sixty who responded to the fantasy survey almost always indicated their fantasies as those of "pure romance." For example, a sixty-nine-year-old widow wrote: "I devour romance novels—the old-fashioned kind—and I really enjoy the classics, like those by Jane Austen. Inside, a woman is never old, and we remember with relish the courting days. When I daydream, I know it is because I miss the special attention I had when I was young and beautiful."

Young, unmarried women who responded to the survey told of many "rehearsal fantasies" that are a normal part of adolescent development. A fifteen-year-old wrote: "Most of my friends agree that our usual daydreams are of meeting that tall, dark stranger, or that tall, blond lifeguard at the beach, and having him fall madly in love. I even daydream about what I will be wearing, how my hair will look, and exactly what I will say to him."

Romance fantasies are often stimulated by romance novels. One possible problem psychologists see for the woman who grows up drawing *all* of her images of love from the romance in novels is that, in most of these stories, the heroine's search for identity results only in her identification with a certain man. Her life is validated only by finding a man worthy of her emotional efforts.

Psychotherapist Joy Davidson of Beverly Hills, California, sees a second, related problem: young women can imprison themselves in a place where love cannot be perceived unless it is accompanied by *turmoil*. After all, to be exciting, the novels must include tension, mystery, and love in turmoil. Women who have been greatly influenced by romantic stories may fail to associate the gentleness of a long-term relationship with true love. Instead, *these women may equate upheaval with passion, and passion with love.* (Dr. Davidson feels that many women who deny they equate passionate upheaval with love nonetheless do, since they are tempted to cast aside established relationships, acting as if relationships that are "comfortable" are therefore "unromantic.")

This most common category of fantasy, that of romantic encounter, shows clearly the greatest emotional need of a woman as a sexual being: *the need to feel that she is attractive and desirable to a desirable partner.*

The second most common category of fantasy is **being courted or pursued by a number of men**. Again, survey responses included many examples:

"In reality I am not a flirt, but in my daydreams I am idolized by a number of men. . . ."

"My daydreams are of the good old days at college, of dating and the excitement of having guys 'fall' for me. . . ."

Daydreams and fantasies in this category are not expressing physical, sexual needs as much as they are emotional needs— the need of pride in a society where a woman's worth is measured largely by her attractiveness, the need to escape boredom and find adventure.

"My husband is a creature of habit," reports a woman from Mobile, Alabama. "There seems to be no spontaneity or creativity in our sexual relationship. Perhaps this is why my fantasies are about different men with differing looks and differing actions. . . . But these imagined suitors all have one thing in common—they all think I'm irresistible."

Other fantasies in this category often stem from a desire to be less inhibited. "I have awakened several times from a dream in which I am dancing seductively before a crowd of men. I know I don't want a relationship with a number of men, but I think I subconsciously want to be freer in my sensuality," says one respondent.

The third most common theme was the *highly erotic and perhaps forbidden*, such as dreams of a relationship with someone who is married.

In general studies, some women admitted fantasies of group and/or homosexual encounters. In Christian circles, the fantasies were much more conservative, but still, one housewife summed up the questions of many when she asked, "Why is it that the forbidden is so exciting?"

Therapist Joy Davidson writes, "While romantic challenge with someone forbidden may produce flashes of powerful, delectable sensation, these challenges give only the illusion of achievement. What most women are really hoping to acquire—self-worth, love, success, happiness—simply cannot be achieved in this way" ("Why Some Women Create Melodrama," *New Age Journal*, October 1988).

We have to realize that a world saturated by mass media is being pushed to the limits of human emotion. Each new TV mystery tries to be more scary than the last, each new tragedy to produce more tears, each new romance to be more erotic. With all of this hype and stimulation, normal emotions can seem dull. The world is caught in the process of "diminishing returns." For the woman who is saturated, the thoughts that once brought sexual arousal are no longer stimulating: she moves further and further into thoughts of the forbidden.

The law of diminishing returns is especially evident to those who have fallen into the addiction of pornography. Once thought to be solely a male addiction, pornography has a hold on many modern women.

"I first picked up pornographic magazines in the homes of the single career gals I met at work," writes a woman from Maryland. "At the beginning, I found the stories and pictures almost humorous, but before long the magazines got a hold on me. It has become a real problem for me. The trouble is, that stuff leads you on. You pump emotional energy into it, but you don't get anything in return like you would in a real human relationship, so you find yourself hungering for material that is more and more erotic. . . ." Her letter went on to describe her experience with the law of diminishing returns in sexual fantasies that are pornographically inspired: "I put more and more energy into this habit, but I get less and less out of it."

The fourth most common theme is *violence or forceful seduction*.

One twenty-eight-year-old wife and mother reports having repeatedly had a powerful fantasy about being spanked and roughly treated, until she recognized, through counseling, its roots in early childhood. "My father was a difficult man and I could never be close to him. He left my mother and me when I was four years old, and before that the only time he paid attention to me was when he spanked me. I was terrified at the time, of course, but that was the only relationship I had with my father. I can't tell you how helpful it has been to look at my sexual fantasy objectively, from the eyes of an adult who was still reacting as a child." This woman's fantasy did not indicate she actually wanted to be mistreated. The same is true of fantasies of rape.

Rape fantasies often represent a way of avoiding responsibility for sexual needs. Some women were raised in an atmosphere that made them ashamed of strong sexual feelings. A California woman shares, "My mother said that we women did not need or desire sex as much as men do. But in my fantasy I don't have any choice, I am not responsible for the action and I might as well enjoy it."

Unlike rape, which is an act of violence, rape fantasies tend to be overlaid with romantic images; they are more like *seduction* than actual force. As researcher Kathryn Lance points out, "This is almost always the basic sequence of events in any historical or contemporary romance novel—the dashing hero forces himself upon the unwilling heroine who initially resists, only to surrender later in a swoon to his torrent of kisses."

The romantic component is evident in a bondage fantasy reported by a single woman named Jane, a thirty-eight-year-old Wall Street executive. "I've had fantasies since I was a teenager about being tied up," she says. "Once I'm helpless, my handsome captor is free to do anything he wants." The erotic component is only a part of her daydream, however. "For me, the important thing is that my attractive lover wants me. He ties me up because he cares for me so much that he can't let me run away from him."

Will fantasies of submission disappear as women become more assertive in real life? Dr. Levay feels that such fantasies will diminish but will never completely disappear. Even men commonly have fantasies of submission. "There is a desire to relinquish control," he says, "to let someone else make the decisions. As modern women have become more powerful in their real lives, they may more frequently find themselves desiring an escape in fantasy from their real-world responsibilities."

Though the prime purpose of sexual fantasy is stimulation, many fantasies also provide release from anxiety. Even non-sexual fantasies often revolve around the desire to escape the pressures or responsibilities of the real world. A mother of three preschoolers writes, "My current favorite daydream is simply one of hours spent alone exploring a tropical island!"

Sexual fantasies also make up for deprivation in real life. Lindsy's husband has a new job which includes long sales trips. "When he is gone, I daydream about him, just as I did when we were dating!" she writes. This creates what Dr. Goldberg calls "a delicious longing." This "delicious longing" echoes the feelings of the Shulamite lover in the Song of Solomon: "On my bed night after night I sought him whom my soul loves. I must arise now and go about the city, for I must seek him whom my soul loves."

Interestingly, however, studies show that women who are

apart from their husbands do not necessarily fantasize more than women who are actually with their mates. This illustrates the fact that the "delicious longing" created by a focused sexual fantasy is important on a *day-to-day basis*, and once again reminds us that the mind is necessary to feminine sexual fulfillment.

Anticipation is one of God's greatest gifts. Charlie and Martha Shedd, in their classic book *Celebration in the Bedroom*, write about the part anticipation plays in their happiness together after many years of marriage:

> I want to think of sex as God first thought of it—a gift to celebrate, excellent in every way.
>
> During the day, we think, "I can hardly wait. Tonight we celebrate."
>
> What will she be wearing? One of my favorites, or nothing? How will she want me? Aggressive? Slow and sensuous?
>
> Where will he want me? Upstairs? Downstairs? Somewhere on the carpeting? Which of our many ways? Softly, easily, laughingly, gently, violently?
>
> For the wise, talking about sex ahead of time, gradually turning up the thermostats, can be a great part of great sex.
>
> The Bible says, "Where there is no vision, the people perish." (Prov. 29:18) One modern translation has it: "Where there is no forward look, the people become discouraged." Ditto for sex.

Rachel is a young wife who wrote that in the past her fantasies had occurred during only part of her monthly menstrual cycle. "My problem was that I didn't often think about sex and it seemed like my husband never thought about anything else. So I actually forced myself to think 'sex,' and it's amazing how many sexual images there are in the world if you look for them. I made myself a sexual person. I believe you can do that. By concentrating, you guide yourself into thought processes that make you that way. I had not been turned off by sex, just sort of blah during most of the month. So if there are women who wonder, can I make myself sexy, I know you can. And if you ask my husband, he would say, 'You sure can, thank God!'"

TO SHARE OR NOT TO SHARE

Our daydreams and imaginations are clues to our inner wants and needs. Some women are fortunate enough to have the quality of communication in their marriages that enables them to share these needs with understanding husbands. The three women quoted below wrote about the benefits of sharing:

"Joe and I have been married for eight years and have a wonderful friendship. Recently I have realized that my sexual desires were stronger than ever, and even though our communication is open and honest, I felt a little awkward about sharing my inner changes with Joe. Since I did, his response has been wonderful. He said, 'You'll never know how much it means to me to know that you need me more than ever.'"

"In my fantasies, I was much more daring, much more enticing than I had been in real life. In reality, I was pretty self-conscious and afraid of being laughed at. When I finally shared my daring fantasies with my husband, I became much freer and less inhibited in real life."

"My fantasy has always been one of being romantically pursued by an imaginary Prince Charming who is consumed with love for me and gives me his undivided attention. I finally opened up and told my husband these dreams about a man willing to 'climb any mountain, swim any ocean' to show his love for me. Well, of course my husband can't be that way all the time, but he has become much more demonstrative of his love for me."

Often, however, women are *not* able to share their innermost thoughts. In our survey, a surprising 52.5 percent were not comfortable about sharing sexual fantasies with their husbands.

In the previously mentioned survey from Columbia University, a full two-thirds of the women surveyed said that they *rarely or never* share their private sexual thoughts.

One reason women might not share their fantasies with their husbands was given by a woman quoted in Chapter 2: "It would hurt him terribly if he knew I daydreamed about one of his close friends."

Other women have a relationship in which, because of hurts in the past, sharing on this level seems too risky. Others report that their husbands are men who are "just plain hard to talk to."

Men encounter this same difficulty in sexual communication. Dr. Timothy Boyd, a clinical psychologist in Oregon, reports, "Time after time as couples have sat in my office for counsel and I have asked the husband to talk about his sexual needs and longings, the wife has later commented to him with surprise, 'Honey, why didn't you tell *me* these things?'

"'I don't know,' he usually answers, 'I guess I just felt embarrassed.'"

Maybe in your situation you feel you have *no one* you can talk to about your inner thoughts and fantasies. And there are times when *all* of us have experienced failures in our attempts to express our dearest longings and our deepest needs.

Yet there is counsel available for each of us. There is a Friend who listens to our questions—more than that, He welcomes them. He understands our needs because "He became flesh and dwelt among us." He is our High Priest who is able to feel total empathy for the human situation.

We seldom have the courage to come to God with questions about our sexuality. Why? We need not draw back in embarrassment from the One who knows us better than we know ourselves.

> *Lord, you have examined my heart,*
> *And know everything about me. . . .*

When far away, you know my every thought.
You made all the delicate inner parts of my being.
You knit me together in my mother's womb.
Thank you for making me so amazingly complex!
It is amazing to think about—your workmanship
   is marvelous.
                                    —Ps. 139:1–2, 13–14

Maybe your husband or a friend has asked at some time, "Why are you so complicated? I have a hard time understanding you!" Maybe, in frustration with your own feelings, you have asked yourself the question, "Why am I so complex?"

The truth is that human complexity is the crowning glory of creation. No other creature, however beautiful, comes close to the awesome mental ability, emotional capacity, and spiritual intensity woven into a physical body that exists in the human being.

In Ps. 139:14, we have read the words of King David who understood that the intricacy of human nature is by divine design. David wrote, "Thank you for making me so amazingly complex! It is amazing to think about—your workmanship is marvelous."

Our intricate design, even the amazing complexity of human sexuality, is a wonder that shows the divine genius of the Creator. The next time someone says, "You are so complex," you can respond with a smile, "Thank you! God made me this way."

With our questions and our frustrations, we can follow the advice of Jesus, who said, "Search the scriptures, set your heart to seek and understand God's wisdom, for in this you discover eternal life, a life that is full and free" (John 5:39; Amplified Bible). In Scripture, there are *over 450 references to our minds and imaginations*.

There are many other verses which speak specifically of our sexuality. (For example, the eight chapters of the Song of Solomon give many examples of what marriage therapists would call "sexual technique." Ephesians, chapter five, and Colossians, chapter three, talk about the sexual fulfillment husbands and wives are to give to each other. The book of Proverbs gives many verses of wisdom about being "continually enthralled with the mate of your youth" and avoiding sexual temptation.

Then, there are even verses like Deut. 34:7, which is the final statement made about Moses, the greatest of Old Testament leaders. In the King James version we read, "When Moses died, his eye was not dim and his natural force was not abated." Many Hebrew scholars agree that the phrase "and his natural force was not abated" literally meant "and Moses was still *sexually potent*." We would blush to think of complimenting a spiritual leader in this way, but the Bible is graphically honest in portraying sexuality as part of God's good plan!

The book of Isaiah gives us a name for the Lord that personifies a special aspect of the relationship we can have with Him. In Isa. 9:6 we learn that "His name shall be called the Counselor."

As we turn from the common themes of romantic and sexual fantasy in this chapter, to some of the needs behind our fantasies in the next, we will begin to consider the unique, personalized wisdom that is available for every individual from the eternal Counselor.

Chapter Four

Through a
Glass, Darkly:
The Need Behind
the Fantasy

COUNSELORS and analysts
tell us that a woman's most constant romantic fantasies and
daydreams are often indications of her inner needs. It is obvious, however, to both Christian and secular counselors, that
even though a fantasy may indicate inner emotional needs,
fantasy alone cannot meet those needs.

Dr. Peter Dally, a highly respected London psychiatrist and
senior consultant at Westminster Hospital, expresses the despair of many professionals who deal with individuals whose
fantasies have raced out of control: "I have dealt with a lot of
problems by asking about fantasies. I have seldom met the
needs behind those fantasies, and therefore the problems remain." Dr. Dally's words reflect those found in 1 Cor. 13:12,
where human insight is likened to "seeing through a glass,
darkly . . . we see only in part, we know in part."

A California housewife writes of her personal frustration: "I feel as if I am caught on a treadmill. I know that some romantic fantasies are simply because of physical, sexual need, but I must admit that I spend a great deal of time in romantic fantasies and daydreams. After a while my daydream grows boring and I go on to other fantasies that are more sensual and exciting. I feel like I am searching not just for sex, but for more fulfillment, but I am not getting it."

How then can a woman's emotional needs be met? Is there an answer to the cry of a woman's heart for love, for meaning, for excitement, for fulfillment?

Daydreams about our feminine sexuality flow out of very real physical and emotional needs. Unlike other physical drives (such as the need for food and sleep), human sexuality is incredibly complex.

Your sexuality is woven into all parts of your physical anatomy—from the pituitary gland beside your brain, to the ovaries and reproductive organs, to the hormones that flow throughout your body, to the skin itself as an extension of your central nervous system. As if this weren't complicated enough, your sexuality is woven through your mind and intertwined with your emotions. It is a thread braided throughout the core of your being.

Human sexuality is so complex that even the experts—the doctors, the scientists, the therapists—who have spent their entire lives studying the subject must throw up their hands in amazement at how limited our comprehension of it ultimately is.

Research and surveys have, however, outlined several needs that reveal themselves repeatedly in feminine sexual fantasy—needs that are not only physical, but also emotional. The most common category of feminine fantasy, that of pure romance, shows the greatest emotional need of woman as a sexual being: **the need to be cherished.**

1. I NEED TO KNOW I AM WANTED AND CHERISHED

This need is, undoubtedly, the most urgent emotional need of every infant ever born, whether male or female. Each child has a desperate need for love and acceptance, which are the foundation for our self-worth. And in women, this emotional need becomes interwoven with sexuality. Like men, a woman may experience arousal based on physical attraction, but generally a woman needs to *build her fantasy around a partner who wants her for herself as well as for her body*.

Recall that in our survey, women often fantasized not only that their partner was treating them differently, but that they themselves were different! "I can't imagine my husband desiring me the way I look sometimes after a long day with the children," one woman confided. "In order to enjoy myself sexually, I imagine that I am a gorgeous redhead, and another time that I am a blonde femme fatale." These daydreams are born out of a woman's desire to feel more attractive and therefore more highly prized and loved.

It is a wise husband who comes to understand this crucial aspect of a woman's sexuality. When a woman sighs, "I long for romance," she is saying *"I long to be pursued because it shows me that I am lovable and desirable."*

Reader's Digest carried a delightful story from a South Seas island where women were valued according to how many cows their husband had paid as a bride price. In "Johnny Lingo's Eight-Cow Wife," Johnny had paid eight cows, a very high amount. Johnny's bride had not been considered beautiful. Yet when the author met her, she struck him as the most beautiful, sensuous woman he had ever met. "I loved only Sarita," Johnny told the author. "Think of what it means to her to know that she is worth so much to me. I wanted an eight-cow wife." Sarita's confident beauty flowed from realizing the high value she had for Johnny. Being "an eight-cow wife" assured her that she was lovable, and she became breathtakingly beautiful.

The Creator understands this feminine need for cherishing, and sets a divine standard for tenderness. Throughout the New Testament, we read that He views His people as a beloved bride. In Hosea, we see that it is His desire to draw us to Himself "with tender cords of love." In the Song of Solomon— that three-thousand-year-old romantic classic—the Shulamite is smitten with her lover because he draws her by "words which drip honey" about her beauty and charm. (The Middle East still uses Solomon's chapters as a marriage manual for teaching romantic and sexual technique.)

Most men are verbally expressive during courting—at least they give it their best shot. One woman lovingly and laughingly included the following memory in her response to our daydreams survey. "On my first moonlit walk with the man I would later marry, he gazed at me earnestly and said, 'Lois, *you look just beautiful in the dark.*' I laughed right in his face— but I knew his intentions were good! He never has had a 'way with words.'"

Somehow the John Wayne, macho man-of-few-words has survived too long in the Western world to be easily cast aside. Many husbands sink slowly into this image of manliness, becoming more and more awkward about expressing themselves—unless a wife can help them to see how her sexuality is woven into her self-esteem and that her self-esteem is reinforced by both words and actions.

One Anchorage, Alaska, woman realized after a hard year of marriage, in which she was "tempted to look elsewhere for romance," that she didn't really want to get out of her marriage—she wanted to put something into it:

"I wrote a letter to my husband, using my best calligraphy, which included the words of that old song, 'Try a Little Tenderness.' You know: 'Women get lonely . . . try a little tenderness.'

"I also wrote in the letter how much I loved him and wanted

romance with no one but him, and that for me romance meant communication. A few days later I gave him the most helpful book, *The Lonely American Male*. At the end of this year, I looked back and saw that romance is coming back into my marriage, because I am feeling loved.

"My husband doesn't always remember to tell me when I look appealing, or which of my outfits he finds especially alluring, but he is making a sincere effort. I have learned, to my surprise, that he thinks I am sexiest when I come home from a business meeting dressed immaculately in a suit and heels. Some husbands may find their wives more appealing in tight jeans, but Joe said, 'When you are in your office clothes, you look so sexy to me because you look so intelligent, so classy, a woman worth conquering.' This meant the world to me because my career is important to me, but I never really knew Joe found me sexually appealing in this role."

This woman, like many of us, feels that feminine romantic feelings are tied to sensing that we are desirable. But how can we expect men, who are by nature less verbal than women, to say what we need to hear unless we are willing to be more communicative? As reported in the last chapter, many women have been afraid to share their deepest longings. Even in this "liberated" society it is hard to be "liberated" around those we are closest to. But women who risk openness are often surprised at the understanding response they receive.

A woman from Atlanta wrote, "We had been married for five years before I told my husband of my secret dreams of a golden-tongued Romeo type who told me constantly of his adoration. My husband is finally realizing that, for me, a large part of my romantic and sexual fulfillment comes from the things he *says*. Before that he was caring, but very inexpressive. As I have told him about my longings, he has been more honest about his own, and we have become much closer. When we are making love, he tells me when I give him ecstasy, and this heightens my passion."

Another woman wrote, "Embedded in my mind is the picture of a shining knight who swept his lady off her feet and carried her to his bed. Now my husband had only done this the night we were married. Recently I sheepishly told him this, and since then I have been scooped up and carried off to bed from all parts of the house!"

Then there are those sad confessions from women who say, "No matter *what* my husband says or does, I just don't *feel* loved."

The women who express this sentiment are giving voice to a far deeper need than any romance could ever meet. While they say "I don't feel loved," they may actually be expressing a thought from the subconscious mind: *"I don't feel lovable."* Expecting the right romance to completely meet the needs of self-esteem is an impossible dream.

> *Love is an ideal thing,*
> *marriage a real thing,*
> *and confusion of the real*
> *with an ideal*
> *does not go unpunished.*
> —Goethe

IMPOSSIBLE DREAM #1: **"The perfect relationship will meet all of my emotional needs."**

The simple truth is that *no relationship* can meet *all* of your emotional needs.

One woman learned this the hard way: "The day my husband left me, he told me that I had drained him emotionally dry. He told me that I was like a reservoir that was empty and that he had poured all the love in me that he had had to give. I knew he was right. I have been like an emotional leech. He could never do enough to convince me that I was loved, but I didn't see it until it was too late."

Another woman shared what she had learned during marriage counseling several years ago: " 'There is absolutely no hope for our marriage,' I cried to the counselor. 'My husband is a doctor, and we are in two different worlds. He is so busy in his work, he has no time left for me and the children. My whole world has been wrapped up in him, but I'm tired of sitting home and waiting for him. I'm not accomplishing anything on my own.'

"I expected the pastor to empathize with me, but he said, 'Young lady, you're not a whole person. You're just half a person. You cannot survive if you depend on someone else for all of your happiness. You must *become a whole person* and quit depending on your husband or someone else to make you happy.'

"I was embarrassed and angry, but I knew he had hit the nail right on the head. I left that office convinced that I had to step out of my role as an emotional cripple, and find my own source of happiness through the inner healing of the Lord."

Bill Gothard, whose Institute of Basic Youth Conflicts has thousands of enrollees each year, says, "*Most unhappiness is the result of trying to meet all our needs through human relationships.* For example, the husband comes home from work tired and grumpy and feeling a need for understanding from his wife. But his wife has her own needs. She is feeling frazzled, lonely, and she wants him to lift her spirits. They lean on each other. The unspoken message rings out, 'I'm hurting, honey; heal me. I'm down; lift me up. I'm depressed; make me happy. I'm in need; meet my need. Put your arms around me and love all the hurt out of me.' "

Of course, neither of these individuals can meet *all* of the needs in the other, because some needs are spiritual, and only God can meet those needs. As one housewife wrote on her fantasy survey, "*You can be in the arms of someone you love all night long and still wake up crying inside.*"

The greatest hindrance to having our fantasies and expectations met is often not the man we are with. The greatest hindrance to feeling loved and cherished is often the scars we carry from childhood.

Dorothy Briggs, author and child psychologist, has completed voluminous studies on self-esteem. She writes, "The key to inner peace and happy living is high self-esteem, for it lies behind all successful involvement with others."

When children are unsuccessful in building self-esteem, they deal with feelings of inadequacy in one of three ways. They (1) erect defenses—working out various coverups for feelings of inadequacy; (2) submit—accepting their "inadequacies" as a fact of life and leading self-effacing lives; or (3) withdraw—retreating into a pattern of fantasy.

The adult woman who is not a whole woman can dream of romance all day every day, but *she will not find it until she finds healing for her self-esteem and self-worth.*

The beautiful phrase from the book of Genesis, "Two shall become one flesh," does not mean that two halves come together to make a whole. A fulfilling romance happens, rather, when two whole people "become flesh" in the intimate sexual relationship that God intended.

Many women are in need of deep inner healing of their self-esteem which will lead to emotional wholeness. Then, a wife will not be like the woman who wrote, "My husband could never do enough to convince me that he loved me." Instead, she will be able to receive the love that her husband offers, believing him when he says "I love you," and not viewing him in terms of that impossible dream in which he meets all of her emotional needs.

IMPOSSIBLE DREAM #2: **"The perfect man" is out there somewhere!**

A single teacher from New Orleans wrote: "I am often emotionally and physically attracted to a man who I think is ideal, and then when we start to date I find I am disappointed in him. I am still looking for the perfect 'ten' who meets all of my needs and expectations."

Why is this young teacher so consumed in her search for Mr. Ideal? Like so many modern women, she has absorbed the idea that if she can just find the perfect man, she will live happily ever after.

Too often, *we expect perfection in another when we are very aware of our own imperfections*. Like those women who want the perfect relationship, this woman from New Orleans falsely assumes that perfection in another will "fill in the gaps" which keep her from being totally happy with herself.

Other dreams of a "Mr. Perfect" can center around a distant, unattainable figure, and reveal a different emotional need. It is normal for teenage girls to fantasize about idols like movie stars and rock singers. But author Dr. E. Devers Branden tells the story of a young woman named Clarice who, even in adult life, was unable to leave behind the normal teenage fantasies of heroes or idols. If Clarice ever daydreamed about a man she had met, he was always so distant (a bank teller, a casual acquaintance) that a real romance could never possibly begin.

Clarice admitted to Dr. Branden that she was afraid of the challenges of love, afraid of finding out *whether or not she could gain and hold another's affections*. Fantasizing about television or movie stars or fleeting acquaintances is, after all, very safe.

"If we are attracted only to people who are unattainable, we have to look at our fear of intimacy with a real person here and now," Dr. Branden says. In her counseling, she encourages women in this "idealization" category to complete the following sentences:

The good things about being attracted to someone who is unobtainable are ⸺⸺⸺⸺⸺⸺⸺⸺⸺⸺⸺.
The bad things about being attracted to someone who is unobtainable are ⸺⸺⸺⸺⸺⸺⸺⸺⸺⸺⸺.

"Asking myself that last question really turned the lights on in my mind," Clarice told her. "I had to admit why I had been thinking as I did, and I had to realize that, in the long run, my 'idealization' was very destructive. I had to change, or I would never find happiness in reality."

An unsigned response to the daydreams survey said, "I cling to my fantasies of movie stars, even though I'm forty years old. I never was able to gain the love and admiration of my father, and I guess it just feels easier to hold real men at a distance, to relate only to those imaginary lovers who look like the hunks on the screen."

Counselors agree that idealization is a way of diminishing personal anxiety. A woman who must overidealize a relationship lacks confidence in herself and her own individual worth. An example of this is the young "groupies" who follow rock idols. Most "groupies" are girls who, in the trauma of adolescence, derive their sense of self-worth from those they idolize. Of course, most young women gain confidence and outgrow this stage. *The deep need in every developing woman is to understand her own intrinsic value as a unique human being.*

Aristotle knew the truth that psychologists affirm today; he said, "Happiness flows from self-contentedness."

2. I NEED PURPOSE AND DIRECTION

The second most common category of fantasy, that of being loved by many different men, once again often expresses emotional rather than purely sexual needs. "It is not that I have an overactive sexual appetite," one woman wrote on her survey, "but instead of a life filled with the daily drudgery of raising a family, every individual desires a life filled with meaning and excitement."

In our modern youth-worshiping society (a society created largely by advertisers), romantic, sexual love is seen as the highest goal and the crowning glory of life. Because of this, we view the important days of life as those spent attracting and capturing the heart of Mr. Right. The emotional energy put into days of romantic pursuit *can make other days seem less meaningful*. Once one lover is attracted and "conquered," a woman, to find new "meaning," may turn her fantasies toward a new lover.

The Highest Priority of Life?

The modern idea that the most important days of life are the fleeting days of youth contrasts with the belief of past generations that the important days are those of *productive adulthood*. But the modern idea has taken firm hold. An American child who grows up on the standard television diet can easily believe that *the goal of life is romance and that physical attractiveness is the means to this goal.*

Comments from survey respondents make these connections clear:

"When you look at all of the hundreds of novels written for women, it is really hard to find one about a woman doing something other than attracting a man. Where are the novels that deal with the courage, the adventure, the tenacity of purpose, the talent and intelligence that can fill the heart of a woman?"

"I am always wondering if I could get certain acquaintances attracted to me. I long for the good old dating days of college. I am just friendly enough to see if the man will pay me a little extra attention. I didn't think this could destroy my love for my husband, but lately I have been seeing what a deadly game I am playing. New emotional adventure, that's what pulls at me, just like 'the continuing saga' of a heroine in a series of romantic novels."

If we have allowed our fantasy to become that of enticing many different men, we need to rethink our current mind-set. The J. B. Phillips New Testament says it perfectly in Rom.

12:1—"Don't let the world around you squeeze you into its mold!"

The problem with the idea the media convey (that if life lacks meaning you need a new romantic relationship) is that it puts the cart before the horse. In reality, romantic love and *sustained* sexual fulfillment flow out of two people whose lives *are filled with meaning!* Significantly, a main cause of male midlife impotence is the loss of a career or failure of a business. When a man feels worthless and his life lacks direction, his sexual drive often fails. Good sex does not give purpose and direction— it most often flows out of a life made confident by purpose and direction.

A lack of inner direction may not bring about sexual dysfunction in marriage, but it often sets us up for temptation. In a later chapter, we will look at questions about the effect of fantasy lovers on one's real-life partner, but first we must admit that *a great percentage of a woman's boredom with romantic life can come from a lack of purpose and direction in daily living.* And a lack of inner direction sets us up for temptation. . . .

One of the most well-known stories about the consequences of temptation is that of King David and Bathsheba (2 Samuel, chapters 11 and 12). The eventual result of David's affair with Bathsheba was that he planned the murder of her husband and "a sword entered his household," with his children observing violence and ultimately becoming violent against one another.

Where did this tragedy begin? From 2 Sam. 11:1, we learn that "at that time of the year when kings go forth to battle, David remained at home." One day, from the roof of his palace, David "cast his eyes on Bathsheba." His idleness in a time when he was accustomed to direction and purpose may have been the factor that set him up for a fall. His life lacked the direction it once had—he fantasized that a new love would be the answer.

The tendency to fantasize in times of idleness was commented on by a survey respondent: "There are some times when I am much more absorbed in romantic fantasies than others. After stopping to think about my daydream survey, I realized to my amazement that my fantasies are seasonal. During the spring and summer, the children and I are out and active. We have a huge garden and I coach tennis, and we find a hundred fun things to do. During the winter I spend a lot more time indoors, and I am realizing that my fantasies become my great companion. In the winter, I feel addicted. . . ."

In *Harper's Bazaar* there was recently an article entitled "Sex: Can It Cure Arthritis?" Obviously we live in a time when we think that sex is the answer to everything. Hugh Hefner is only one of many who have made a fortune telling us that the satisfying of sexual urges with different partners is the main purpose for living.

But Jesus said that man cannot live by bread alone—or solely by giving attention to the physical. The purpose of our existence is far greater than the great American fantasy machine would have us believe.

The Westminster catechism says it simply and beautifully: *"The chief goal of man is to love God and enjoy Him forever."*

Can the goal of "enjoying God" add to our human sexuality? YES! Because that purpose brings back the joy of life itself, and we will discover that *"He has richly given us all things to enjoy"* (1 Tim. 6:17). We enjoy all of life, including the gift of our sexuality, when we allow Him to bring purpose and meaning to daily life, when sexual fulfillment does not become the goal of life, but the natural result of a life finding wholeness and purpose.

> *Thou hast made us for thyself, O God,*
> *And the heart of man is restless*
> *until it finds its rest in thee.*
> —St. Augustine

3. I NEED ADVENTURE AND EXCITEMENT

The third most common fantasies are those characterized by eroticism and adventure.

Even in lives filled with purpose and meaning, we must face the routine, the repetition of daily tasks, the ongoing rhythm of "what must be done." How do you deal with the familiar? Have you allowed your sexual relationship to settle into such a pattern that it is no longer vital and interesting? Are you liberated only in your fantasies, and still inhibited with your flesh-and-blood lover?

Most experts, whether secular or Christian, agree that too much time spent in fantasy is not emotionally healthy. Dr. Peter Dally, of the Westminster Hospital in London, has found in his counseling that "*99 times out of 100, sexual problems are caused by a person's inability to associate his or her youthful fantasies with his or her adult partner.*"

In a loving, trusting relationship, a man and a woman can learn to be liberated not just in sexual fantasy, but in reality. Respected seminar leaders Charlie and Martha Shedd often share with others the insights about sexual fulfillment that they have gained through their many years of marriage. They write, "Great marriage is letting each other into the deep places. It is for opening doors that have been closed for a long time, secret doors [fantasies]. . . . Great marriage is saying, 'Let's look in here together.'"

Martha shares the humorous story of being with a Japanese Christian friend and seeing a book entitled *100 Positions for Sex*. Her friend said, "That's wrong. I was taught that there are sixty-five positions . . . the others are all just a variation." Martha laughs, "I thought I had been creative —I realized we might have something to learn from other cultures, and *there is still uncharted territory ahead of me!*"

Author Marabel Morgan (*The Total Woman*) has been teasingly accused by talk show host Johnny Carson of encouraging women to meet their husbands at the front door dressed only in Saran Wrap. That idea is not in her book—but a lot of other great ideas are! She stresses that we should use imaginative ways to add zest and adventure to our sexual relationships with our husbands.

Of course, in the family setting, this kind of erotic abandon takes planning and timing! This is, perhaps, the area in which most wives fail miserably . . . *planning* and *timing*.

Joann, a young mother of three, writes: "My problem is that it takes a lot *less time and energy to imagine* something highly erotic than it does to actually do it! I need to push myself to lay aside my laziness, because the reality of an erotic experience with my husband is certainly *more lasting* than a wispy daydream."

Joann's statement gets right to the core of the problem in many a woman's erotic sexual adventures with her husband: the problem of time and physical tiredness. She may meet her need for adventure in fantasy simply because fantasy is less physically demanding.

In his best-selling book *What Wives Wish Their Husbands Knew About Women,* Dr. James Dobson attributes much frigidity in women to the "tired housewife syndrome." He writes, convincingly, that fatigue is the number one cause of the average couple's lack of sexual satisfaction.

Ann Marie, happily married for sixteen years, gave this advice in responding to the fantasy survey:

"Too many women expect their husband to come up with the bright ideas for vacations and romantic getaways. Now, my husband loves to get away with me—but if I didn't help him block the time out on his office calendar, if I didn't search for travel deals and make the reservations, we never would have gotten around the block! *Wives are the key to helping their husbands find time for romance.*

"And I am not talking about a great deal of expense. Some

of our most idyllic moments have been in a tent pitched by an isolated mountain stream."

Even the intimacy in the Song of Solomon did not happen by accident. In chapter 2, verse 10, Solomon remembers, "My lover spoke and said to me, '*Arise, my darling, and come away.*'"

If the answer to some of our erotic needs for adventure and excitement has to do with finding the time and physical energy, then *we can take concrete steps toward meeting these needs*. And that, my friends, is encouraging!

Meeting our need for sexual excitement does not involve attracting new partners, but rather, discovering how to *capture the ongoing, ardent passion of the one we love.*

The ancient wisdom of the book of Proverbs says it so well: "The foolish woman tears down her home [marriage], but the wise woman continues to build it by her own efforts" (Prov. 14:1).

4. I NEED TO "OWN" MY SEXUALITY

The fourth area of feminine sexual fantasy deals with being sexually forced or overcome. In Chapter 3, we reported that many women have at times had seduction fantasies.

This category of fantasy can stem from two subconscious factors: first of all, *a longing to have a strong, virile partner*, and second, a desire to be unaccountable for strong sexual feelings.

Occasional fantasies of being "overcome" by a strong sexual partner may have a simple physiological source. The desire to have a strong, virile partner is fundamental to feminine sexuality. This is partly *biochemical;* the sex drive, even though we do not stop to think about it, is biologically programmed for the preservation of the human race through strong offspring. For the sake of future generations, *we subconsciously desire a strong mate*. Human sexuality, even feminine fantasy, is woven into biology and is part of God's larger plan. Therefore, it is physically natural to desire a strong, virile partner, even when procreation is the furthest thing from the conscious mind.

For some women, however, the image of being sexually forced or overcome may be the central theme of sexual fantasy. Women who must always fantasize about being forced or overcome may be suffering from *a false guilt about the strength of their sexual desire.*

Perhaps the woman's main role model, her mother, conveyed a distaste for the intimacy of the male-female relationship. Or perhaps the mother made statements such as "My dear, men have much stronger sexual drives and needs than women," and the girl feels guilty when she discovers that, to the contrary, her sexual desires are strong. Or perhaps false guilt about sexuality stems from a misunderstanding of God's view of sexuality. "When a person comes from a narrow, somewhat rigid, conservative background, there may have been direct and indirect messages about the sinfulness of sex. A woman may lose sight of the fact that it was the Creator who made her to be a sexual being.

If you doubt this, consider the fact that one part of the female anatomy, the clitoris, serves no other function than to give women a sense of pleasure in sex. Obviously, God made sex to be enjoyed." (Randy Alcorn, *Christians in the Wake of the Sexual Revolution.*)

These women need to understand what the eternal Counselor teaches us through God's word about the strength of sexual desire.

Insight from the Counselor

"In the beginning" . . . was sex!

Following the creation of Eve, God saw all that He had made and said, "It is very good." In the Hebrew text, this verse does not just say, "It is good," but "It is very good. It is completely good."

"To understand the Old Testament input regarding human sexuality, we must understand the Hebrew view of the human person as an *integrated whole.* The Hebrews never divided people into body and soul, as did the Greek dualists, or into body, soul, and spirit, as some do today. Rather, the Hebrews thought of a person as a unity. The physical, emotional, and spiritual were various dimensions of a person, but they were closely related and were often used synonymously or interchangeably." says Dr. Sam Middlebrook, biblical scholar and professor of Hebrew literature at L.I.F.E. University.

What was included in that which was "very good" about human beings? Masculinity. Femininity. Sexuality. Sex.

The marvel of creation culminated in the man and woman's sexual union. "For this reason a man will leave his father and mother and be united to his wife, and they will become one flesh" (Gen. 2:24). Genesis 2:25 is the last account of a world without sin, a perfect world, and it says "the two shall become one flesh. And the man and his wife were naked together, and neither of them was embarrassed or ashamed."

Charlie and Martha Shedd offer a wonderful prayer at the beginning of marriage conferences:

> *Lord, help me to think of my sexuality as You think of it,*
> *As a gift to celebrate,*
> *Excellent in every way.*

Throughout the Bible there are verses about human sexuality as a part of God's good plan. Scripture is incredibly candid and honest in dealing with feminine sexuality. In Prov. 5:15–20 and throughout the Song of Solomon, a husband is given advice about how to keep his wife romantically satisfied. In the New Testament, 1 Corinthians, chapter 7, verses 2–5 and Ephesians, chapter six, give practical advice for continuing sexual happiness in marriage.

Besides being created as a good gift, for our good pleasure, human sexuality is the way God has chosen to let us partner in the very act of creation. Through the one-flesh relationship, we are entrusted with the creation of children. And God says, "It is good. It is very good."

This understanding of the goodness of our sexuality meets the deepest need that lies behind many "seduction" fantasies—the need to admit the strength of one's feminine sexuality. *The strength of sexuality is a gift from God.*

THE OUTER LIMITS

Sometimes, however, sexual fantasies that lodge in the psyche go beyond the norm, beyond what is wholesome and emotionally healthy.

A survey respondent included with her daydreams survey a note about the catharsis of dealing with a harmful sexual fantasy:

"I know that many women dream of being overcome by a strong, virile man, but my fantasies went far beyond that, into the 'outer limits.' I can't share all of the details of my growing up, but I'll just say that I saw things when I was a child that made me believe that sex should be forceful and violent. After several years of marriage, these mental scenes were all that seemed to make me sexually aroused, and I could not break my lifelong pattern. Because my husband was not forceful, I fantasized about other men. There I was with a good husband and yet daydreaming about criminal types. . . .

"When I became a Christian, I decided to honestly face these fantasies. I had to hold them up to God and cry out for deliverance. Old thought patterns are not easily broken, but God is doing a miracle in me. He is showing me that *my sexuality is to be upbuilding and fulfilling and not a quality for degradation.*"

Some marriage therapists may say, "Your sexual imaginings

are harmless, totally harmless. You can think about whatever turns you on." But others believe that our thought-life affects all other parts of our being.

Christians are not alone in acknowledging the spiritual reality and power of the imagination. Owners of new age bookstores promote titles like *Wishcraft: How to Get What You Really Want*. Even cult leaders like Anton Levey, author of a satanic manual, write, "Imagery becomes the formula which will eventually lead to reality."

Our fantasies *do* eventually affect our lives.

What wisdom about the "outer limits" of sexual fantasy do we find in Scripture?

Insight from the Counselor

As we have discovered, *God is not against sexual pleasure at all—what He hates is the misuse of sex and sexual fantasy*. Phil. 4:8 gives us His guidelines for our thought-life; we are to "think on these things . . . whatever is pure, whatever is lovely. . . ." In Hebrew, the word "pure" means wholesome or healthy, unpolluted, untwisted.

In Prov. 4:23, we are counseled to guard the thoughts of our hearts, "for out of them flow all the important aspects of living."

Probably the best-known scripture that refers to sexual fantasy comes from the words of Jesus in Matthew 5:28. He said that lust, or sexual craving, with the wrong focus, is sin. When we use the word "sin" in this book, we need to understand the meaning of the Hebrew word for sin—*hamartano* —which literally means "to miss the mark; to miss the target." Jesus was teaching that sexual fantasy is wrong when it focuses on the *wrong target*. On the other hand, sexual longings *can be* "*on target*."

Prov. 5:15–19 gives us the target for which we aim: "*Be continually enraptured with the love of your chosen mate*."

As one woman discovered, *"God is showing me that my sexuality is to be upbuilding and fulfilling."*

"You cannot say that your physical body was made for promiscuity. It was made for the Lord, and the Lord is the answer to all its needs" (1 Cor. 6:13; J. B. Phillips).

OUR GREATEST TREASURE

God designed you, your spirit, your soul, and your body. In the Bible there is a clear demonstration of His concern for all of your needs: spiritual, emotional, and physical.

The Bible is wonderfully practical because it speaks to the whole person. It contains a wealth of wisdom that applies to our emotional and physical longings. The Bible speaks about human sexuality with such candor and honesty that it is clearly the instructions of a loving Father concerned about *every aspect* of His children's lives.

The Bible is also filled with a wealth of knowledge about the "inner you." Over 450 verses refer to the mind and over 150 to the imagination. Countless other verses deal with troubling mental images, such as those of fear (see Chapter 8). Still others give the how-tos of self-control that are the building blocks of the "fortress of your mind" (see Chapter 10). In every aspect of living, we are offered the help of the Counselor.

Romantic sexual fantasies are a normal part of our human sexuality, and our sexuality is woven into the very core of our being; we cannot separate ourselves from this integral part of our personality. But while some would say, "Set your imagination totally free," the Bible gives guidelines and shows the importance of having a mind that is in control.

Daydreams and fantasies are expressions of one's inner needs and desires.

In the fourth chapter of John, we read the story of Jesus and the Samaritan woman at the well, a woman with inner needs. In her conversation with the Messiah, she discovers that He knows her—He knows that she had been married five times in vain attempts to find fulfillment. Jesus tells her, "I can give you Living Water, a source of satisfaction so deep that you will no longer be thirsty."

Her response? "Lord, give me your Living Water!"

Jesus looked past the obvious problems of her life—the string of broken relationships and her confusion about spiritual reality. He saw her inner needs. So many of us come to God with our "problems," but His desire is to touch us deeper—to touch our inner needs:

> our need to accept our sexuality as a gift,
> our need to feel wanted and cherished,
> our need for feminine fulfillment,
> our need for purpose and meaning in our daily lives.

Chapter Five

The Fair Exchange

"No flesh-and-blood man can be expected to live up to a fantasy."

In a case study included in Chapter 2, Summer O'Brian came to this conclusion. She then went on to ask the earnest question being asked by many other women, *"Give me reasons, real reasons. Why should I give up the perfection of daydream lovers for the imperfections of reality?"*

In previous pages we have presented the forces, both internal and external, that are pressing modern women to a preoccupation with fantasy and daydreaming. We have looked at common fantasy themes and at some of the needs behind our sexual fantasies. But Summer wanted more than statistics in answer to her honest question.

There is an old saying that some things are "as easy as taking candy from a baby." Now, any parent knows that this saying is absolutely nonsensical—taking candy from a baby is almost impossible! A mother who attempts to take candy away from her toddler is asking for a full-scale war. The child will clutch a gooey handful of sweets with every iota of strength in her little body. She will use tears, screams, pitiful expressions, heartrending sobs—and even the run-and-hide technique if these stand-and-fight methods fail.

No, taking candy from a baby is not easy. A well-seasoned parent will tell you that there is really only one way a very young child will give up the candy in her possession. You must offer her something better. You must make a fair exchange.

None of us is really very far removed from the little child who clings with determination to a bit of candy. Our mental habits and imaginings are closely guarded possessions. We will not give up the sweetness of a fantasy, however small and worn and soiled it may have become, unless we have concrete reasons.

Some fantasizing is normal, but when does the gossamer world of fantasy become harmful? In this chapter, we will consider six possible side effects in the life of one who clings to fantasy, side effects that will help us to see how giving up fantasy for romantic reality can be a fair exchange.

1. EMOTIONAL ANESTHETICS

"I'll admit I'm hooked on television sagas like 'Dallas' and 'Dynasty,' " Elaine said after completing the daydreams survey, "and I am a gothic romance addict. After all, I am an emotional creature and I want to experience the *full range* of my emotions."

How surprised women like Elaine are to learn that too much vicarious living actually acts as an *emotional anesthetic*, dulling our true emotional responses and narrowing our range of feelings!

Since Ivan Pavlov won the Nobel Prize in 1904 for his experiments in "conditioning" the responses of animals, countless other scientific experiments have proven that we can condition our central nervous system to specific reactions.

Each time we get emotionally involved in a show or movie, at the end we must wipe our tears and tell ourselves not to respond emotionally. We are slowly but surely conditioning ourselves toward emotional numbness.

Watching a lot of television removes us from real life. The effect on children is especially disturbing. A cartoon in the *New Yorker* several years ago pictured a father changing a flat tire on his car in the driving rain while his two children watched him through the car windows. "Don't you understand?" the father was saying. "This is *life*; this is what is happening. We *can't* switch to another channel!"

Neil Malamuth, professor of psychology at the University of Southern California, is especially concerned about the desensitizing of teenagers. "The clearest effect we are seeing of teenage TV viewing is a desensitization to violent images; they become less emotionally reactive. It may lead young people to be slow to respond to violence in their own environment. It tends to make them hardened in other ways as well—emotional ways."

This points out a truth that affects us all, young and old alike. As one teacher stated in her fantasy survey letter, "I have trouble . . . dealing with real people after watching a few hours of television. I suppose it's because there was no effort while I was watching. Dealing with real people always requires a bit of effort." And let's face it, human nature can be lazy and choose the easy way. The way of no effort.

A Physician's Observations

The physicians serving the emergency room at a Los Angeles hospital were the first to document the phenomenon.

"Have you noticed that people have changed emotionally in the last few years?" Dr. Leland Brown asked two of his colleagues one evening as their shift in the emergency room drew to a close. Graying and fatherly, Dr. Brown had fulfilled his once-a-week assignment as directing physician in the hospital's emergency room for twenty years.

"Actually, I'm referring to the emotions of those who bring patients in for treatment," he continued. "It seems to me that there's been a decline in empathy levels, in people's ability to respond when a loved one is in pain."

"I know what you mean," replied Dr. Harold DuVale. "I've noticed some emotional change over the years, especially in women. For example, tonight I set the fractured arm of an eight-year-old boy. The boy had been brought in by his mother. I'm sure that she loved him, but she seemed somehow *distant* as we talked about his injury. . . ."

"Yes, that's what I mean," Dr. Brown continued. "It goes beyond a person's desire to act calmly during a crisis. It's as if some people are unable to feel the reality of the situation touching their family member."

"In some, I've noticed what I call 'emotional distancing,'" Dr. James O'Conner said, entering the conversation. "But I've also noticed women *overreact* when they bring in a patient. Their actions and words are so dramatic that they seem almost, well, . . . phony. They're reacting, and yet their reactions seem lacking in feeling."

"Can we be coming to a time when the men and women of American society have a decreased capacity for *true emotion*?" Dr. Brown asked his friends. "And if so, what's behind this emotional change?"

This conversation led the three physicians to begin a research project which would last for ten years. From 1965 through 1975, they surveyed individuals who brought patients to the hospital for treatment. During this same period, their survey was given in several other hospitals across America. The results of this study, although not conclusive, do point to some trends in the emotional patterns of our society.

"One of our most startling conclusions came from our questions about television and other mass media," Dr. Brown reported. "The amount of time an individual spends watching television, movies, or involved in a fantasy world seems directly related to that individual's ability to respond emotionally in real life.

"For example, a woman who watches soap operas or sad love stories for several hours each week finds herself getting emotionally upset. Then she must tell herself, 'Don't be upset, after all, that didn't really happen.' Without knowing it, she is actually *conditioning* her responses. Then, when crisis strikes in real life, she finds herself unable to truly respond. The reality seems to be *only another story*.

"Her feelings have been anesthetized."

2. THE BLOCKING OF COMPASSION: BONNIE'S STORY

Bonnie's experience was a concrete illustration of the physicians' observation: her feelings were anesthetized, and as a result, she was unable to offer the priceless gift of human compassion. Bonnie included the following letter with her survey.

"When my twin sister, Debbie, was going through a horrible divorce, I found that I was saying all of the right things as I offered verbal sympathy, but without true feeling. I felt as if I was acting out the *role* of a loving sister. Deep inside I wasn't really feeling her pain. One day I said to myself, 'Wait a minute: this really is *happening*. Debbie is my real sister, my twin who means the world to me. Her divorce is real and it is breaking her heart.'

"That night I visited my sister just as I had been doing but the tears I cried weren't crocodile tears. Debbie called me later to tell me this was the first time she had felt truly comforted during the entire crisis. She said that after my visit she felt lighter, and for the first time, felt a tiny ray of hope.

"That was the first time I realized that my years of television watching were affecting me. You see, I had seen so many divorces on the screen, from 'Days of Our Lives' to 'The Way We Were,' that Debbie's real-life crisis seemed like just another script. All of the 'fantasy crises' had blocked my feelings of compassion when they were needed in a real crisis."

Is it possible to walk through times of grief with our loved ones and never truly empathize with them? Is it possible that we can rob those we love of a priceless gift—the strength they gain from true empathy?

Is it possible for an anesthetized woman to even "act out" her *own* crisis experiences, walking through reality but not in it? Can an emotional stupor keep her from throwing herself 100 percent into *dealing* with that situation so that it can be *changed*? Can it prevent the crisis from becoming an avenue of personal growth for her?

Sadly, all these things are possible. If our emotions are continually aroused by unreal situations, if we continually tell ourselves "Now, don't get too upset, what you're seeing isn't real," then our emotional response system becomes terribly confused.

Brenda returned her fantasy survey with this sorrowful story: "When my husband told me he was thinking about leaving me, I should have *responded* with anger, or with tears, or with some real feelings. All I felt was numbness. I had wrapped myself in a cloak of unreality, so much so that the real world just didn't seem real. I didn't respond when I should have. . . ."

And, if our ability to respond to crisis has been dulled as we have watched acted-out grief on the screen, our ability to respond to violence has been equally affected.

Former Surgeon General C. Everett Koop feels that surveys about apathy toward violence have shown that some people do not respond to help victims because they simply "cannot believe that what they see is really happening." In a 1983 address entitled "Violence on Television," Dr. Koop told a horrible true story about a young girl in St. Louis who was raped in a public fountain while people walked by, unresponsive. Finally, a little boy jumped on his bike and rode to a policeman for help.

One bystander later gave a pitiful and profound reason for his unresponsiveness: "I guess I passed by in a stupor. I have seen so many fights and attacks and muggings on television . . . it just wasn't registering that this was for REAL."

In 1988, a mother in Oregon watched as her neighbor's child was being kidnapped by a stranger in a Safeway parking lot. "The little child was screaming for help, but I was in a daze. It seemed like I was just watching it on TV or something—I wasn't frozen by fear, I just couldn't seem to realize that this was for real. Thank God, a young clerk ran out of the store and tackled the abductor, and the man was arrested. When it was all over, I was screaming at myself mentally, 'Respond, damn you! When it's real, you have to RESPOND.'

We can't be emotionally dulled—we *need* to be emotionally alive. We must be able to respond, quick to respond. This means we must remove the roadblocks that stand in the way of the compassion our friends and family so desperately need. We must realize the price that is paid by those around us if we have been emotionally anesthetized and experience the blocking of true emotions.

3. ROBBED OF GREAT TREASURE

One of the most wonderful abilities of the human mind is that it can solve problems creatively. In science, the five steps of creative problem solving make up the basis of all research. Mankind's technological progress is the story of the solving of one problem after another. This "problem solving" use of fantasy, this "inventive imagining," is a potential treasure for every human being.

Yet if the strength of the imagination is that it can enhance reality, the danger is that it can be used to avoid unpleasant reality. In this way, one's dream world can steal away the joy of the real world. The woman who does her living in her imagination is not only anesthetized to emotional realities, she is robbed of the very fiber of her life. As C. S. Lewis wrote, his concern was that in the twentieth century, romantic fantasy may be the only way we use our imaginations.

The following stories are examples of women who are being robbed, in different ways, of the joy of the unique reality that God gives to each of us.

Carmen's Story

"I am writing to you because the fantasy survey that I saw in a magazine really hit me. . . .

"I have always done a lot of daydreaming. Back in high school I daydreamed during many of my classes because, at least during the last years, the lectures were so absolutely boring. I could easily keep up my grades by doing my homework, so I developed the ability that many teenagers develop— the ability to look like I was listening while really I was being charmed by the prince of an imagined kingdom.

"Well, I'm not a teenager anymore. I'm a mother with two toddlers, and I have a nice husband. But let's face it, the chores of mothering little ones are pretty routine. And I find myself daydreaming quite a bit. The daydreams are not usually sexual, but they are always romantic. Sometimes I dream about college days when I was dating. After all, the time of life that's the best is when a couple is being attracted to each other and falling in love. . . .

"But here's the problem. I find that the constant demands

of little children really bother me, because they are always interrupting my thought-life. For example, if I am at the sink washing dishes, I'll start daydreaming, and I find that I push the kids away if they come around with their chatter. I know I shouldn't do this. I even find myself sitting them with a pile of toys in their room so they'll 'leave Mamma alone.'

"Then recently an older neighbor that I really love came by for a visit and she said, 'Oh, Carmen, you are in the most wonderful time of mothering! The memories I have of my children as preschoolers are my richest treasures. Why, we made mud pies together and built tinker-toy cities and sailed kites. . . .'

"While my neighbor talked, I knew she meant it, and I realized that I am not storing up many memories like the ones she has. Besides that, my two little guys aren't storing up many memories of these preschool days with Mom.

"I want to break out of my mental patterns, because I see that I am being robbed of some special joys that will never come again. I am being robbed of my *time*. And there must be a lot of others like me. . . ."

There *are* others. One anonymous young mother sent this poem with her survey:

> "*My husband sits behind the Great Wall of Newspaper,*
> *My children go together to Nintendo Land . . .*
> *Good—*
> *   I am left alone with my Fantasies.*"

Mary Lou's Story

If Carmen was being robbed of the joy of quality time with her two little boys because of her fantasies of the days when she was dating, Mary Lou was having her actual dating years stolen from her because of her imaginary life.

Slightly overweight when she entered high school, Mary Lou managed to gain thirty-five pounds before graduation. By the end of her sophomore year in college, she had added forty more. She never dated but made it clear to her friends that that didn't bother her.

"My older sister, Clare, knows me so well," Mary Lou shares. "She was the only one who could've confronted me about my weight problem and about my lack of concern for my own health.

"One day Clare sat me down and said, 'Mary Lou, you're a beautiful girl, but your weight is covering up your beauty. I'm worried about you because you don't even seem to try to diet or exercise. Your health is at stake. You never go out with a guy . . . '

"'I don't care,' I interrupted, getting huffy. 'I don't need dates all the time like some girls we know.'

"'No, you don't need dates with the guys from college.' Clare raised her voice. 'That's what bothers me. You don't need relationships with real guys 'cause you always have your nose stuck in some romantic novel. I'm afraid you're living in daydreams! And while your head's in the clouds, *you're missing a wonderful time of life*. Wake up, Mary Lou!'

"Well, I stomped out of the room we shared in a rage—a rage of embarrassment because my sister had hit the nail on the head. That night through many tears I came to the truth about myself: my weight and my lack of male admiration had been of no great concern—as long as I spent plenty of time in the world between the covers of a good novel.

"As I devoured the latest dime-store romances, I always pictured myself as the heroine, sometimes tall, blond, and svelte, sometimes dark and petite, but always gorgeous. I had a few friends who were anorexic but wouldn't admit it, and I thought they were crazy. Yet here *I* was, overweight and unhealthy, yet refusing to come to grips with that fact!

"Oh, the torture of those next few months. The torture of honestly looking at myself in the mirror, of beginning to pick up a tennis racket instead of a book, of starving my body of physical cravings for too much food, and saying 'no' to emotional cravings for the comfort of my imagination.

"One thing spurred me on. Clare was my roommate and therefore my watchdog. I wanted to prove to my nagging sister that I did not have my head 'in the clouds.'

"I call what I went through withdrawals, withdrawals from old eating habits and old thinking patterns. But after a month or so, I actually began to feel better. Clare had been right (darn it)—my health had been at stake and I hadn't even noticed. And real life was passing me by.

"*I had been wasting all my creativity on fantasy,* instead of using my mind to solve the problem of my weight, instead of developing relationships with the men friends around me. The season of life for real dating was being stolen away."

Rosemary: "The Child Split Apart"

Mary Lou was blessed with a family member who loved her enough to challenge her withdrawal into fantasy. Rosemary did not have this blessing.

Rosemary was demure, reserved, and meticulous about herself and her clothes. As a young child she was timid, and her parents did not force her to mix with others. She read a great deal, and as she grew older, her ideals were always based on fictional characters, who seemed much more glamorous than ordinary people.

When Rosemary went away to a large university, she became terribly unhappy. At home she had had a room of her own, but in the dorm she shared a room with two other girls. Her roommates and classmates sensed Rosemary's withdrawal from them and labeled her "stuck-up." She slept poorly, did not exercise or eat correctly, and took less and less interest in her environment. One morning she simply did not get up.

She was taken to the college infirmary, and she soon required more help than a baby. She was as motionless and stiff as a mannequin. Food placed in her mouth was not swallowed; she had to be fed through a tube. When her mother arrived, Rosemary did not recognize her. To her mother, the most startling aspect of Rosemary's condition was that an attendant could place her limbs in any awkward position and they remained fixed. Her eyes gave only a vacant stare.

To her mother's horror, Rosemary was diagnosed as having a form of schizophrenia, the most common form of insanity. Dr. S. I. McMillen, author of *None of These Diseases,* reports that 50 percent of the beds in all American mental hospitals go to schizophrenic patients.

Patients arrive at this illness in different ways, but of Rosemary, Dr. McMillen says, "Long before she became mentally ill, her world was split between a pleasant fictional world of glamorous people and the unpleasant world of reality.

"Schizophrenia can be a specific reaction to severe anxiety arising from inability to meet the demands of normal adult adjustment," Dr. McMillen reports.

"Some young people are unwilling to put forth constructive efforts to adapt because it is easier to get themselves away from the work of real people by withdrawing into the twisted spirals of their fantasies," reports Dr. William S. Sadler.

This observation is echoed in the words of many women who noted on their fantasy surveys, "It is easier to flee to the world of fantasizing than to deal with flesh-and-blood people." Some young women must be especially careful to live in reality; their emotional health and future may depend on it.

DONNA'S STORY

Fantasy robbed Donna of the most intimate moments of her life, as she explained in this letter which she sent with her survey:

"When my husband and I were first married, I felt pretty awkward and inhibited, and I wasn't really finding much sexual fulfillment. But I loved my husband very much, and so early on I sought counsel. The therapist encouraged me to fantasize so that I could be more relaxed when my husband made love to me. The advice worked—I imagined I was being kidnapped like some Helen of Troy by a swashbuckler who couldn't live without me, and I was able to come to climax.

"But several years later, long after I had lost my initial shyness and inhibition, I realized I was always in a fantasy when my husband made love to me. One night I thought, *My God, if there were a terrible accident tomorrow and I lost Jerry, I would not have clear memories of these intimate times with him. I haven't BEEN here!*'

"How diabolical that I had noticed so little about this flesh-and-blood man who shares my life. It was high time that I lay aside my old continual 'romantic turn-on pattern' for the real romance that was right before my eyes.

"I came to my senses one day when I read a parable. I am including it in the hopes it will awaken other women. This parable is actually the true story of a Persian man named Ali Hafed. . . .

"Ali Hafed owned a very large farm with orchards, grain fields, and wonderful gardens. He had many camels and holdings and was wealthy and content. One day Ali was visited by an old Buddhist priest, who sat by the fire and told him of the beauty of strange gems called diamonds. 'They are the most valuable treasure of all,' the old man whispered. 'Like captured rays of sunlight. Nothing has value above that of diamonds.'

"Ali Hafed began to dream about diamonds, about how much they were worth. He became, in a very real sense, a poor man. He did not have diamonds, and he grew greatly discontented. He had not lost anything, but he felt he was lacking.

"One day he said, 'I will have a diamond mine!' He sold all that he possessed, left his family in the care of a neighbor, and began his search.

"Hafed traveled throughout Palestine and northern Africa, searching, but finding no diamond mine. At last, after his money was all gone and his health was ruined, he stood on the shore at Barcelona, Spain. A great wave came rolling in, and the discouraged, suffering old man could not resist casting himself into its pull. He sank beneath the ocean's weight and died.

"The man who had purchased Ali Hafed's farm led his camels to his garden brook one day to drink from the cool, pure water. As a young camel put its nose into the shallow water, the owner noticed a curious flash of light from the stones in the white sands of the stream. As he stirred the sand with his hands he found scores of priceless gems: diamonds.

"That was the discovery of the most incredible diamond mine in the history of mankind, the Golconda. The largest crown jewels in the world have come from that mine.

"The pitiful thing is that Ali Hafed's jewels were right before his eyes, but he didn't realize it. My sexual fantasies have been like counterfeit gems, when I can reach out for the real diamonds. *I can have the precious memories of really being with my husband during lovemaking.*"

4. ISLANDS IN THE STREAM: FANTASY AND ISOLATION

In the letter just quoted, Donna wrote that she didn't have the precious memories of intimate moments spent with her husband because she had never really been there.

Do husbands sense this emotional distancing? Many men say that they do. In a song from his album, "Dreamland Express," John Denver put it poetically. He asks his lover if, while she is physically with him, she is really with *him,* and not just living in a fantasy.

Judith, a housewife who has the blessing of a loving and perceptive husband, wrote:

"My real struggle with an indulgence in fantasy living has come in midlife, when the children were gone and when I felt the impact of fading youth. I have a loom in my home and my crafts give a nice second income, but while my hands have been busy my mind has been filled mostly with daydreams.

"One day Jim looked at me sadly and said, 'Judy, I feel like we are out of touch with each other. I don't know how to explain it, but I feel like you are being wrapped in layers of translucent material or something like that. You're here, but when I look into your eyes, you're distant. I touch you, but I don't feel like I'm touching you.'

"I was amazed when Jim expressed these feelings. I started to pray about it and think about it, and I realized that day after day I have been wrapping myself in a cocoon of my own making. And that cocoon was shutting Jim out.

"I remember one time in art school when the instructor asked us to paint our version of a fantasy spirit. I did a watercolor of a queenly creature in the brightest colors of the spectrum, with streams of bright color flowing from her in every direction.

"If I were to paint a fantasy spirit again, I would do it much differently. The colors would be muted, like the landscape is in an autumn fog that subdues the golden colors of October, and the spirit would be trailing long pieces of filmy gauze, which would float down over figures that were still and unmoving. Some of the figures would be so wrapped in the filmy material that you could no longer see them, and they could no longer see out. *Fantasy wraps us in cocoons*."

Judith reports that in the months since determining to not grow isolated from Jim, she has come to a new definition of the word "meditate."

"I always had thought that meditating was clearing one's mind out. That is the way the Eastern religions teach meditation. But the word 'meditate' in the Bible and in Jewish tradition is the word 'hâgâh.' It means 'to murmur' or, more properly, 'to mutter knowledge.'

"When the people of the Old Testament were meditating, they were actually repeating scriptures, quietly remembering the Torah.

"Nowhere does the Bible say, 'Empty out your minds.' It says instead that our minds should '*be full!*' When I sit at my loom weaving, I no longer spend hours on fantasy. I listen to tapes of good books (the classics), and I have some tapes of the Bible. I was one who thought I had no time for learning . . . I just wasn't using the time that I *do* have!"

Judith, a talented artist, wrote that she would paint a picture of fantasy as a spirit that was wrapping individuals in a filmy, gauzelike material—individuals still partly visible, but obscured in a fantasy cocoon. A woman named Darcy included a different mental picture of fantasy in a note with her daydream survey:

"Some may picture sexual fantasy as a beautiful thing, but to me it became as ugly as a tapeworm in my brain, growing to fill more and more of my mental capacity, until there was little of *me* left. I was like a zombie. Here in body, but isolated and distant. I thought I was doing okay until my husband threatened to leave me. 'Even though I am married,' he said, 'I feel so alone.'"

His feelings recall the *Newsweek* article quoted in Chapter 1: "Where does [all this fantasy] leave modern men and women? . . . On separate but equal Fantasy Islands."

5. FANTASY AND THE LAW OF DIMINISHING RETURNS: TRUDY'S STORY

As we have seen, studies have shown that too much vicarious living can actually bring about a dulling of our senses. It is also clear that while fantasy dulls us, it eventually becomes dull in itself, and sadly unfulfilling.

"I have discovered that my sexual fantasies were addictive," confided Trudy, a New York career woman. "They 'led me on.' My fantasies which had once been exciting became dull, and I found I was fantasizing about things that were more and more 'way out.' Now I understand why they say that pornography can be addictive."

Any sexual fantasy will eventually become dull. Why? Because it is one-dimensional and lifeless, and therefore inherently subject to the law of diminishing returns.

The law of diminishing returns says that for any amount of expended energy, the results will be progressively less. For example, a ball bounced against pavement will rebound 80 percent on the first bounce, 60 percent on the second bounce, and so on. Eventually, the ball stops bouncing altogether.

This is why pornography, even "soft" pornography, is so addictive. A thirty-two-year-old man from Washington, D.C., wrote one of the most touching letters of all of those that arrived with the survey:

"Pornography? I didn't choose to call it that. Men's magazines. Gentlemen's entertainment. Articles and stories for the man-of-the-world business executive that I was becoming. Things I should read and see because 'everyone else is seeing them.'

"But pornography has a terrible hook. It seems like a little thing when you first swallow it, but it catches you and pulls you out into deeper water.

"Before I knew it, my old fantasies didn't fulfill, and I found myself fantasizing about younger and younger partners—fed by the pictures of childlike girls in many magazines. . . .

"I feel like I am getting free from the pornography just in time. What I didn't see going into all this is that there was such an *emotional hook* in these things, because old fantasies become dull and less fulfilling, so you are trapped into looking for something more erotic and 'way out.'"

(This man's comments about magazine pictures of children were borne out in a study by Judith Reisman, who found that images linking children with sex occurred an average of 8.2 times in issues of *Playboy*, 6.4 times in issues of *Penthouse*, and 14.1 times in issues of *Hustler*. Reisman reported that adult-child sex is shown as harmless and even glamorous.)

Sexual fantasies diminish in their emotional returns. Why? In her letter, Trudy went on to say, "The fantasies were one-sided. The only way I have any return for the expenditure of emotional energy is when there is a real human being loving me and pouring emotional energy back into my heart."

One unsigned note on a daydream survey agrees with Trudy:

"Fantasies can't escape the law of diminishing returns, because fantasy love is love in a vacuum."

6. THE WINTER OF OUR DISCONTENT

Television and movies present distorted ideas about love and romance, and these distorted ideas often lead to discontent.

Even those connected with the silver screen, including actresses known for steamy love scenes, express their concern about what an overdose of romantic input is doing to this generation.

Joann Phluge, who played a leading role in the movie *M*A*S*H*, said this about her own life: "On stage, soft music starts to play when I walk toward the hero, the lighting is just right to 'set the mood,' and he has just come from a two-hour makeup and wardrobe session. . . . This is the illusion. At home, there is no music, and there has definitely been no makeup session, but when my husband reaches out to hold me, I tell myself 'This is not acting! This is the man that I love.' "

In a four-year study of daytime television viewing, the University of Pennsylvania School of Communications monitored the effects of the soaps on 30 million Americans. Among its findings and conclusions were the following:

• Heavy daytime viewing can distort a viewer's ideas about human sexuality. The data compiled show that soap operas average 2.19 intimate sexual acts per hour! The message is that passionate encounters should occur frequently, if not continually!

• The overwhelming number of televised sexual encounters involved unmarried partners. Dr. Bradley Greenberg, director of the study, placed that number at *94 percent* of the total.

People magazine reported in July 1982, that: "What we have been saying many times a day, every day for the past thirty years is that the goal of life is to *entice someone new*. And kids are learning it's okay to hop into bed with every new acquaintance."

Katy's Story

The contrast between the illusions painted by the camera and the realities that lie behind these illusions can be almost comical. One of the most delightful responses to the daydreams survey came from Katy, a bank teller in Los Angeles. Katy laughingly shared the story of how her own romantic idols were shattered:

Katy was a small-town girl of the 1960s who grew up dedicated to the hunks of the movie screen. Her special favorites were Paul Newman and Robert Redford. "That is," she says, "until I moved to L.A. in the early seventies and got a job at a bank in Hollywood."

The first mirage to dissolve was that of Paul Newman. Katy actually found herself in a cafeteria lunch line near the real Paul Newman one day. "He is shorter than I am," she realized. "I had always envisioned him as massive, at least six-three or six-four. I staggered out of that lunchroom stunned."

A few weeks later, she confided to a co-worker that now she had only one silver screen favorite—Redford—and that she would "give anything to see him in person."

"Why, Katy," her co-worker exclaimed, "Redford has been coming into this bank almost every week!"

"He hasn't!" Katy answered. "If Robert Redford had been in our bank, I would have noticed him. Why, I've seen *The Great Gatsby* five times!"

"He does bank here, Katy," her friend declared. "The next time he comes in, I'll point him out."

True to her word, Katy's friend nudged her one morning as they waited on customers. There, at her friend's window, was Robert Redford. And Katy realized, to her great amazement, that she had seen this man before.

"Seen him, but not recognized him," she writes, chagrined. "His hair was not as blond as I had thought, his skin had some imperfections, and he shuffled in and out of the bank without the hero's swagger I expected.

"My friend looked at my gaping jaw and started to laugh, and then I started to laugh, too. My illusions about the attractiveness of stars like Redford had left me discontent with my life. But now I gasped out the truth: 'Who would've *believed* it! My husband is cuter than Robert Redford!'

"And that's the truth!"

A MIRAGE OR AN OASIS?

In earlier pages we have seen that the human imagination is a wonderful gift of God—a gift meant as a blessing, not a curse. Our creativity exists because we are made in the image of the Creator. There are many positive uses for daydreams and times for imaginings and fantasies, even those that are sexual. Yet many modern women have fallen into the pattern of *using their imaginations for romantic fantasies alone, and of retreating into those fantasies often and intensely*. In their hearts, these women say, "Give me reasons. Why should I give up the perfections of my daydream lovers for the imperfection of reality?"

In this chapter, we have looked briefly at six of the reasons for exchanging fantasy for reality. First of all, too much vicarious living, far from enabling us to use "the full range of human emotions" as one woman hoped, acts as an *emotional anesthetic,* dulling our ability to feel and respond in real situations. Second, women who live in fantasy are sometimes *unable to extend full compassion or empathy* to those around them, for reality may seem like "just another TV show or movie." Third, when we choose to live in a mirage, *real time is stolen away* from us. The real "Days of Our Lives" are taken from us, and we settle for a mirage.

Besides losing the precious moments of real time, we lose the energy that could be used in real creativity, in problem solving, in thoughts which help us to change and better our lives. The real goal of the imagination, said poet Matthew Arnold, is to create "a stir and growth everywhere"!

The fourth reason we should be willing to exchange fantasy lovers for reality is that these mind games can lead to *isolation*. As mentioned in Chapter 3, in adolescent girls romantic fantasies are normal and serve a sort of rehearsal function. But in mature women, the tendency to cling to fantasies tends to detract from a relationship. A husband, for example, may perceive his wife as "distant."

The fifth reason for giving up a preoccupation with imaginary lovers is that "fantasy in a vacuum" is intrinsically subject to the *law of diminishing returns*. A sexual fantasy becomes less and less fulfilling. Soft pornography loses its excitement—we are hooked and pulled along. We experience the truth of the Latin proverb: "The best thing, when used in the wrong way, becomes the most loathsome."

Last but certainly not least, too much fantasizing can leave us discontented and unhappy with our lives. As one woman wrote on her daydream survey, "When I come out of my fantasizing, I feel worse than ever. . . ." As mentioned in the last chapter, fantasy often indicates emotional needs, but fantasy alone cannot meet those emotional needs. In obsessive fantasy, we lose sight of the value of the life that God has given us, and the value of the real individuals who fill our lives.

In the world of modern technology, a cubic zirconium can appear larger than a diamond, and just as glistening. Yet any woman with understanding will choose the diamond—it is the real gem, the treasure of lasting value. So often, we are tempted to settle for a counterfeit gem, when God wants to offer us the real thing.

We can settle for a cubic zirconium or desire a real diamond.

We can choose to run after a fantasy mirage or to drink at a satisfying oasis.

> *Your eye has not yet seen,*
> *nor your ear heard,*
> *neither has your heart ever imagined*
> *the real things God has prepared*
> *for those who love Him.*
> —1 Cor. 2:9; paraphrased.

Chapter Six

The Winter of My Discontent

No good Christian man or woman gets up in the morning, looks out the window and says, My, this is a lovely day! I guess I'll go out and commit adultery. Yet many do it anyway.

—Florence Littauer

Populus vult decipi, ergo decipiatur. (Latin proverb)
People want to be deceived, therefore they are deceived.

Secular counselors and therapists have made claims about the imagination that are absolutely contradictory.

In the area of sexual fantasies or romantic daydreams, these experts often say, "Think whatever you like. Set your imagination totally free. Erotic movies and books won't hurt you. Just because you imagine certain things doesn't mean they will ever happen."

In 1988, when the President's Commission on Pornography reported to Congress, commission members testified that what we read and see *does* affect us. Following the report, the Playboy

Foundation, a subsidiary of the magazine, began to spend a fortune to convince the public that "mental intake" is irrelevant.

As for the popular press, magazine articles by the score make statements such as the following:

"Fair is only fair. Only a prig would deny that it is time for women to express their sexual fantasies as freely as men. Fantasies are fun, nobody gets hurt and they are even nonfattening! There is no mess, no fear of intimacy . . ." (*Newsweek*, May, 1983).

"It is only natural to have sexual fantasies about the men you know and work with. These are not harmful . . ." (*Ladies' Home Journal*, January, 1985).

On the other hand, well-respected experts talk about the power of the imagination to bring change in other areas of real life! Consider, for example, the mind bank theory of Dr. John Capis, a well-known author and seminar leader. Basically, Dr. Capis's theory is that you are hindered or propelled by all the data that you have fed into your mind bank: "Just as a computer can only print out what has been fed into its memory bank, the human personality can only feed out what is in the mind bank." Success motivators have long recognized the truth of this principle. The first step to success, they say, is to decide what you want to accomplish and when. Identify clearly your goal. Get a mental picture of it. Think about it every day. As you create a clear, strong image in your mind, the appropriate emotions will follow, and your goal will be realized!

How can what we think about affect every area of our lives *except* sexual actions? How can our imaginings about a career bring results, as success motivators teach, but our sexual fantasies have no consequences, as the Playboy Foundation contends?

The contradiction is obvious, and 1 Tim. 6:20 warns us about this kind of illogical thinking: "Avoid the godless mixture of contradictory notions which are falsely called 'knowl-edge'" (J. B. Phillips).

The Bible is clear and logical in expressing the importance of thought-life. In beautiful prose, its wisdom long antedating that of the mental bank researchers, it states:

"Guard your affections with all diligence, for out of these thoughts will flow all the issues of your life" (Prov. 4:23).

"As a man thinks in his heart, so he is . . ." (Prov. 23:7).

Therapists agree that, while visual stimulation affects women, a woman's most important sexual stimulation is men-tal. A woman's mind is part of her sexual equipment, and her body is wired to respond to her thoughts. What a woman sees affects her as she builds a fantasy and develops it.

> The mind is a garden that can be cultivated to produce the harvest that we desire.
>
> The mind is a workshop where the important decisions of life and eternity are made.
>
> The mind is a battlefield where all of the decisive strug-gles of life are won or are lost.
>
> The mind is an armory where we forge the weapons of our victory, or of our own destruction.

What did Jesus mean when He said, "Whoever looks on a woman to lust after her has committed adultery with her in his heart"? Scholar David Hocking gives us a clear explanation:

> First, the word "looks" is in a Greek tense which indicates an ongoing action, a habit of life. I do not believe that it is saying looking with sexual desire at a particular moment in time is wrong. God made us with sexual desire. Men enjoy meeting women and women enjoy meeting men. I believe the passage is a clear warning about centering your attention on a particular person as an ongoing habit. The words "lust for" have to do with concentrating on a certain individual and mentally going to bed with that one.

Dr. J. Allan Petersen, in his excellent book *The Myth of the Greener Grass,* helps us to apply the verse to everyday living:

Suppose I read a legitimate book or magazine, or watch a wholesome television show. Something I see—an ad, a paragraph, a picture—causes a thought of evil to flash into my mind. Is that sin? No. I drive down the street and what I hear on the radio or see on a billboard causes erotic feelings to flood my mind. Is that sin? No. Or while I'm working on the factory line, or in the office lunchroom, I hear the dirty jokes, the risqué cracks, the report of sexual adventures. Is it sin for me to hear it? Of course not.

Or say, as a woman, I meet a man at church who is handsome, kind, vibrant. Though not flirtatious, he has a wonderful personality. A thought flits through my mind that this man would be sexually attractive to any woman. Anything wrong with that? No! It is not a sin to hear the hundreds of transient and tempting suggestions that knock on my mind's door every day, all life long. In the same way, thoughts of selfishness or meanness will flit through my mind.

To the super-sensitive, the devil whispers, "There is something wrong with you. If you were a true Christian, you wouldn't have these thoughts. It's too late, you've already sinned." You can recognize the devil's lies because they are always negative and always lead to hopeless guilt and self-condemnation.

But when that passing thought of evil is welcomed, given hospitality, mulled over and over with the consent of your will, then it becomes an evil thought. If I open the door, warmly invite this stranger in, give him an easy chair to relax in, encourage additional conversation, the stranger has become my friend. This friend now helps me construct a picture—simple at first but ultimately with details and in living color—of all that this friendship can mean to me and the needs that it can meet.

That picture is a fantasy, and fantasies are a preview to the desired action. An affair is experienced many times in fantasy before the time and place of the first rendezvous is set.

A woman's fantasies about a man she knows are often not sexual at first. One woman sent a letter with her daydream survey in which she said, "In the beginning, the daydreams I had about an attractive co-worker were simply ones in which he was complimenting me, telling me I was his idea of the perfect 'ten,' or telling me how brilliant I was. . . ." Then slowly and subtly, romantic fantasies that are nurtured begin to change, to cross the line.

A nurse from Nebraska wrote of a doctor she first found impressive professionally, and then was drawn to him by his gentle counsel to her children. Her thoughts of him grew from respect, to thoughts that overestimated his attractive qualities such as strong masculine leadership. The unrealistic way in which she viewed this man is a perfect example of the progression in many seemingly harmless friendships.

The woman can begin to wonder if the man finds her attractive, interesting, intelligent. She can even begin to plan ways to spend more time with him. All of the while, she can be telling herself, "I'm not doing anything wrong! I'm not sinning!" The needs she wants to meet in this new relationship are emotional and perhaps romantic, but not physical. She is not being, technically speaking, unfaithful.

But is she being emotionally unfaithful to her husband? Won't the quality of her marriage suffer because of it? And hasn't she placed herself in a dangerous position of temptation?

THE SUBTLE SETUP

Christian women are certainly not immune to temptation. As C. S. Lewis warned, "We learn that we cannot trust our flesh, even in our best moments." There are, in fact, some aspects of modern Christianity that may make us especially vulnerable.

Satan is sly with us. He knows that we want to have refined tastes and good motives. He does not tempt us with cheap things or brazen sins, because these would not appeal to our spiritual nature. Rather, he subtly takes some good gift of God, such as intimacy and oneness of spirit and empathy, and interjects into that gift some qualities which are not pleasing to God. He distorts our priorities and tempts us to misuse God's good gifts. In this way, sexual attraction may become a problem in what was a perfectly proper friendship.

In her syndicated newspaper column, "Domestic Affairs," Joyce Maynard usually writes about the kind of affairs that make up a woman's schedule as a wife and mother. In 1987, however, she asked women to write to her about "the other affairs—the extramarital kind." To her surprise, a full three-fourths of the 1,000 women who wrote to her about their affair said that it had begun as a *simple friendship* with a co-worker.

Not only does the work place offer married people the chance to get well acquainted with someone other than their spouse, it is also the place where both men and women tend to reveal their best qualities. "I always look good when I go to work," wrote one woman. "My co-worker has never heard me scream-ing at the kids or seen me in curlers. And I have never seen him slumped before the TV, unshaven and uncombed, for a football marathon. Outside of the home, we tend to put our best foot forward."

Rob Reiner's film *When Harry Met Sally* takes a humorous look at how easily a friendship between a single man and woman can turn romantic and sexual. Actor Billy Crystal as

Harry presented the central theme of the movie when he said, "Sally, for a man there is no such thing as a purely platonic relationship. If a man finds a woman attractive, sex always gets in the way." Reiner was delighted that his movie caused strong reactions; "I like to get people to examine themselves," he said.

For married women and men, the results of friendships that turn romantic are not so humorous. An honest and touching account of how one Christian woman was subtly drawn into an extramarital affair was given in a letter in the September 1983 issue of *Virtue* women's magazine. The letter is included here without editorial deletion, because its words express far more than a mountain of statistics.

One Woman's Response to "The Unmentionable Temptation"

"I just finished reading 'The Unmentionable Temptation' in *Virtue*. As a Christian wife and mother who is now several years on the other side of an affair, there are some things I must say.

"I would warn others that if they first yield to *mental adultery*, it could very easily take them the whole route. If there's time to be alone with the other man, which is often the case when such thoughts persist, the two of you will eventually probably start discussing your feelings with each other, especially if he is a brother in the Lord. You say that you must conquer this thing together with prayer; (what a trick of the devil that is). You will then feel such a tenderness toward each other that you will need to express your affection with some warm embraces. It is a very short road from there to the point where you succumb to more and more sensual temptations and you are no longer trying to resist.

"If you are a sincere Christian, and you have been used to a close walk with the Lord, you will be in for a dreadful battle.

On the one hand, you'll long to go back to really being in love with the Lord. You will wish you could just be interested in the Word again. You will cry over hundreds of songs that used to mean a lot to you, especially "He Is Lord," because you'll know He's not Lord of your life anymore. You will suddenly discover you can not share real testimonies in church or elsewhere, nor share meaningfully with those closest to you. You will waste many precious hours doing nothing but thinking about the affair. You'll find it hard to concentrate on anything else. You will have to keep hiding evidences and that will most likely lead you into lying—another sin you never dreamed of committing.

"On the other hand, you will most likely be experiencing a wonderfully romantic relationship. While it is very sinful, you will be helplessly in love with this man, and completely unable to imagine ending this relationship. Eventually you two will frequently discuss how to stop it. You may even take some painful steps, but seldom will they have any lasting effect. The longer the affair goes on, the more memories you will create and the harder it will be to achieve victory. You will realize then that it would have been so much easier to stop when it was only at the "thoughts" stage. You would give anything to go back and be able to do it over.

"By then, not only will you have lost your closeness to the Lord, but to your husband as well. You will realize to your horror that never, never, never will your relationship with him be the same as it had been. Either you will have to go through the rest of your married life keeping something from him, which you probably never did before, or you will eventually have to confess it to him and hurt him deeply.

"If you somehow manage to get the affair slowed down and eventually stopped, you will probably cry more tears during the next months than you ever have in your whole life. They will be tears of extreme remorse for what you have done to your life, to your Lord, to your husband, to the other man, to your descendants, to your own testimony. There will also be tears of longing as you miss your relationship with the other man. The memories will be your worst enemies. You will wish you could part with them, yet you will cherish and relive every one many times. If you must still have contact with the other man, his presence will be a constant reminder and temptation.

"Eventually, if you hope to regain that closeness with your husband, you will tell him, and it may be the hardest thing you have ever done. The healing of your relationship will be a long, hard road. Again, you'd give anything to go back and do it over. You will long for the days when your husband's lovemaking was the only way you knew, when certain songs, smells, places, clothes, and words did not remind you of the other man. In the strongest way I can say it, you will be sorry, sorry, sorry. Yielding to the excitement will *never* be worth what you will have to reap.

"I am not saying that a person who has had an affair must live in bondage and condemnation the rest of her life. Yes, there is healing of spiritual and marital relationships, even of the painful memories. But it will *not* be easy. If you are at the point of yielding because you think, "Well, eventually I'll repent and the Lord will forgive me, and there will be healing," you are very foolish. It would be thousands of times better to resist temptation at the beginning and never need healing later.

"If you are feeling very drawn to another man, don't discuss it with him. It will immediately create a bond which should not be there. Tell a very mature, but understanding Christian friend, and lick it right then and there.

"Don't have another Christian man as one of your closest confidants, especially if you are in a situation where you two need to spend time alone. Spiritual closeness creates a bond that can subtly lead to physical temptation.

"If you have already yielded and know it must stop, and yet can't imagine how it ever could, take the risk of praying, "Lord, do anything You must to make me be willing to stop."

Then be prepared to take what He brings. In my case, it was a completely unplanned pregnancy. It seemed to be impossible that I could be pregnant by either my husband or the other man because of my ovulation cycle and precautions used. But I was pregnant, and I didn't know by whom. At first I begged the Lord for a miscarriage, but I soon saw the pregnancy as His answer to my prayer. I told the other man and we were dreadfully afraid. We had kept it all so secret, and now what if I had a baby that looked like him? We were both Christians and considered to be very sincere and "turned on for the Lord." We were involved in a ministry, and did not want to bring reproach upon the ministry, and especially not upon the Lord's name. The only conclusion we could come to was to yield to Him, give each other up, and beg the Lord to have mercy on us by letting the baby look like my husband. What an emotionally painful eight months were ahead! Giving each other up was worse than either of us could have imagined. At the same time we could never be sure the Lord would honor us for this painful obedience. What if the baby still looked like him, or was deformed or stillborn?

"The Lord did have mercy on us. The baby was healthy and bore no resemblance to the other man. He has been a tremendous source of joy to our family. When the baby was several months old, I could no longer handle the feelings of alienation from my husband or the strong temptations I had for the other man. I then confessed the affair to my husband. Years later we are still working on the healing of our marriage. Telling him did help me a lot. I knew that from then on, if I wanted to keep from having to hide things from him, or worse yet, having to confess more things to him, I could not yield to any further temptations. Since that time, the other man and I have not discussed our feelings toward each other. It all happened *very* gradually and *very* painfully. I cannot stress enough that even if it is possible to receive forgiveness, victory, and healing afterward, none of that is worth going through the experience. Yielding to adultery, even in thought, should be avoided at *all* costs."

This letter might be the shock therapy that is needed to wake up some readers who are being subtly drawn into an emotional involvement—so subtly that they have not seen where this involvement may lead.

The plain truth is that wedding bands are no insulation against the tug of sexual awareness.

J. Allan Petersen, author and the founder of Family Concern, Inc., makes the following statements about sexual temptation:

1. No individual, however chosen and used of God, is immune to an extramarital affair.

2. Anyone, regardless of victories won in the past, can fall disastrously.

3. The actual act of infidelity is the *result* of uncontrolled desires, undisciplined thoughts, and long-term fantasies.

This, then, is why the Apostle Paul urged us to "cast down imaginations . . . and bring into captivity every thought" (2 Cor. 10:5).

Charles L. Rassieur, a gifted Lutheran theologian, says, "It can be a major turning point in any marriage when both partners discover they can be sexually attracted to persons other than their spouse. This learning about their own human nature can crush some idealistic views about what it means to be in love and married, but then it leads to a deeper level of commitment and love." Rassieur voices an important note of caution. He says, "This is the kind of subject which both husband and wife must be equally willing to talk about. One partner may find it too threatening or distressing to talk about often. This is the kind of communication which must be done with great sensitivity."

KNOWING HIS VOICE

The most diabolical of all delusions, the most unfair and the most destructive, occur when our spiritual enemy plants a thought in the mind of an individual and then convinces that individual that the idea is from God. We must remember the words of Jesus in John, chapter 8: there is a spiritual enemy who is "the father of all lies," "the father of delusions."

Nancy had been married to Phil for seven years and was the mother of two small boys when she found herself tremendously attracted to a single man who served as an assisting minister in her Congregational church. She struggled with her strong feelings for several months before going to her senior pastor for counseling.

By that time, Nancy had begun to believe that *God* was telling her that Phil was going to die and that their pastor friend was to be her new husband. "These feelings are God's way of preparing me," she thought.

In the counseling session, Nancy admitted that she had begun to withdraw her affections from Phil as a result of believing that something was going to happen to him. As so often happens when we bring an inner thought or scheme into the light and share it with a prayerful confidant, Nancy began to see that God does not speak this way to His children. Nancy's pastor said, "The Holy Spirit is not the voice of *fate,* of what *has* to happen. If God forewarns, it is so we will go to prayer!" A biblical example is when God showed the prophet Jonah that destruction was ahead for Nineveh. The Lord spoke this so that Jonah could speak to the citizens of Nineveh and the citizens could turn to Him in prayer. In this way, the destruction was *avoided*.

God does not negate present reality with a mirage of the future. Nancy realized that God wanted her to be "continually enthralled by the mate of her youth," as Proverbs says.

By thinking her feelings for the other man were divinely

inspired, Nancy had relieved herself of all guilt and had not even tried to resist the attraction. Realizing the mental trap that had been set for her, Nancy began to discipline her mind. "My marriage was being ruined, even though the single pastor never said more to me than a kind 'Good morning, Nancy.' Ruined because I had stopped nourishing the relationship between Phil and me."

Nancy chose *not* to share the delusion with her husband, believing that Phil would be deeply wounded and never quite at ease in their church again. She was able to move past her temptation, and she and Phil are happily married today.

Looking back, Nancy says, *"I can't believe that I ever thought God would put such ideas in my mind.* I had not been hearing the voice of the Lord at all! I was helpless until I learned the principle of James 1:13. 'Let no one say when they are tempted, I am tempted by God. . . . He tempts no man. But everyone is tempted when he is drawn away by his own desires and enticed.' "

The Holy Spirit enables us to resist an isolated sexual temptation by considering the *totality* of life—family and fidelity, home and community, the covenants of our past and the building blocks of our future.

"If only I had controlled my desires and taken time to look *into the future,"* laments a woman from Minneapolis. "Several years ago I ripped apart the Christian home that I had put so much effort into. I left because I was so attracted to an acquaintance that I was sure that marriage to him would bring continual romance and emotional highs. If only I could have seen that the fires of passion would cool in this second marriage, too. I ripped up my home and children. I changed my circumstances, but I am in the same place of discontent of heart that I was in before. I feel like I am in the winter of life again. I think now that springtime could have come, and it could have come with my first husband if my eyes had not been looking elsewhere. . . ."

Even in her book, *My Secret Garden* which urges women to set their fantasies free, author Nancy Friday included this honest report from a woman who had pursued her sexual fantasies: "Sexual fantasies, when lived out, are very disappointing. I know that from experience."

This woman is a living illustration of the ageless truth of Prov. 14:1: **"A wise woman continues to build up her house, while a foolish woman tears hers down by her own efforts"** (The Living Bible).

The young woman named Nancy mentioned earlier found strength as she heard God's voice through His word: Let no one say when she is tempted that the temptation is from God . . . we are tempted by our own desires. Another woman who found strength from God's voice in His word is a popular Christian soloist. She and her husband make their home in Hollywood, where their musical gifts have earned them Grammy awards. This entertainer wrote on her daydreams survey:

"I love my husband, but there was a time when I was very attracted to a musician in one of our bands. But I knew that the Bible counsels us to 'Cast down wrong imaginations.' I also discovered the verse that tells us to 'stand firm' in what we know is right (Gal. 5:1). Another version says 'Hold steady.' I would like to share with women that they must just 'hold steady' when temptations come, because *temptations will pass*. I decided to 'hold steady,' to not be alone with that musician, to not nurture fantasies. Now, a few years later, whenever I see that person, I can't believe I was *ever* attracted to him!"

THE CHALICE IN YOUR HANDS

Temptation grows best when unadmitted and pushed into the basements of our minds. It flourishes in the dark atmosphere of embarrassment about our sexuality. It grows in stale marriages and unfulfilled personalities. It begins to die when honest acknowledgment, examination, and confession take place. It wilts in the sunlight of prayer with a caring friend and communion with family. Its seductive power depends on the darkness of a life not illuminated by the light of the Holy Spirit shining on God's word.

Illumination can come from such graphic pictures as the one given in 1 Cor. 10:21. Earlier in the chapter, Paul has begun a teaching on temptation (verses 12 and 13). Then in verse 21, he says "Be careful lest you drink a cup of demons."

One day last summer, my four-year-old, Sammy, marched through the garden to where I was working in the hot sun. "Have a drink, Mommy," he said, and proudly held out what I thought was a cup of cool water. I held the cup to my lips, then gasped. Sammy had apparently left this cup of old Kool-Aid outside for several days. There was mold around the edges, and floating in the cup were several dead ants and some of the yuckiest grublike worms I had ever seen. I shivered to think that, in my thirst, I had almost taken a drink before looking into the cup!

Another lesson in motherhood!

That simple event was a graphic illustration of the warning in 1 Cor. 10:21. You may begin to drink from a cup that looks enticing and realize just in time the horror that the cup contains.

A woman's emotional and sexual needs can create a great thirst. We each have two cups set before us from which we can drink.

One is the chalice filled with undisciplined fantasies and unchecked actions. From the outside, it appears beautiful and desirable. But before your thirst pushes you to lift the chalice and drink, look closely into the contents. Mixed into this drink are seeds of destruction, spiritual parasites, the contamination of what the Bible calls "a cup of demons."

The other exquisite chalice is filled with "the best wine," pure and costly like the miracle wine Jesus provided for the wedding feast in

Cana of Galilee. "*Drink from the fountain that is blessed, and rejoice with the husband of your youth. . . . Let his affection fill you at all times with delight, and be infatuated always with his love*" (Prov. 15:18–19; RSV).

Perhaps for some this image of choosing between two cups, one of them "a cup of demons," seems too strong. But as Dr. Scott Peck says, "the spirits of lust unleashed in our time are strong spirits—we must give strong answers."

SAFETY SIGNPOSTS

One of the most beautiful spots in the entire world is California's Yosemite valley. During a hiking trip there you will encounter many warning signs:

Do Not Leave the Path
Beware of Bears
Falling Rocks
Do Not Go Beyond the Barrier to View the Waterfall:
    Many Have Been Swept to Their Death

But there are other signs, too:

Scenic Rest Stop
Photographic Viewpoint
Historical Marker
National Monument
*** Attractions

In the words of Dr. Petersen, marriage is like a trip through an awesome national park—"a long and memorable journey, if we only obey the signs that are there for our protection."

After years of considering the causes of damage to countless marriages, Dr. Petersen gives warning signs that are posted beside the pathway of marriage. Among them are:

#1. *Consider first your friends.* "In a society where flirtation is the norm and an affair is accepted behavior, you must choose and cultivate friends carefully. Friends who treat marriage infidelity lightly or tell suggestive jokes and stories are really enemies of your marriage. Avoid them. Since many affairs take place between close friends—couples who have had strong friendships together—loose sex talk breaks down the protective walls, piques the curiosity, and encourages fantasies. The more open and transparent the friendship, the more necessary to keep conversation on a high level. Many a woman has faced the double tragedy of her husband's unfaithfulness with her best friend. Without appearing self-righteous or preachy, you can always find ways to let your friends know that you consider fidelity to be very important. And, of course, your own positive actions must support this, so your friends see and hear that you admire, appreciate, and love your partner. When anything is said in conversation that in any way makes light of marriage, you should respond with something positive about your own relationship. Don't let the atmosphere remain poisoned with the doubts and negativism that give marriage a bad press. Be more than a silent witness. Speak up for marriage—for your marriage!"

> *"My eyes will be on the faithful {to their vows}*
> *that they may abide with me,*
> *And he whose walk is blameless will minister to me.*
> *The one who practices deceit will not be welcome in my house,*
> *The one who speaks harmful things*
> *will not be my close friend"*
> —(Ps. 101: 6–7).

#2. *Avoid traps on the job.* It is no secret that many affairs are spawned in the office or that sexual favors often influence contracts and promotions. One attractive and very competent secretary told me how she protected herself. "I turned down all invitations for private luncheons with men in our office— and there were many of them—because I knew myself and I knew it would be difficult not to respond to the admiration of other men. I value my marriage too much to expose myself to those risks."

"Wisdom shouts to you for a hearing. . . . He will help us to make the right decision every time. Wisdom and truth can enter the very center of your being, filling your life with joy. Daily wisdom is far more valuable than precious jewels" (Prov. 1:20, 2:10, 15; The Living Bible).

#3. *Avoid the magazines and entertainment that lower inhibitions.* Take TV soaps, for instance. Dr. Petersen believes it is impossible to build a great marriage and be a devotee of soap operas. Their distorted drama of romance, sexuality, and infidelity encourages comparisons and dissatisfaction. Unconsciously you begin wondering why your spouse is not like "John's other wife" or "Mary's secret husband." Such fictional comparisons are bound to result in a feeling that you're being cheated in your marriage and that an affair would bring release from your boredom. This unrealistic fantasy increases any marital disappointment you already feel. You blame your partner for letting you down. Blaming your partner causes you to become passive in your marriage-building efforts. The result of this decreasing commitment and effort is further marital deterioration. This then further feeds the fantasy and sets you up for an affair. It's a vicious cycle. You cannot build a real marriage on a fantasy with imaginary characters.

The Bible speaks to this area of modern living. Jesus said, "The eye is the lamp of the body. If your eye is good, your physical being will be full of light" (Matt. 6:22).

And Psalm 101: 2–3 specifically helps us consider the media input we allow into our home:

> *"I will walk in my house*
> *with a blameless heart.*
> *I will set before my eyes*
> *no wrong thing."*

(New International Bible)

Margaret Hess, a Detroit pastor's wife, has some practical suggestions for avoiding your own traps, and we give her suggestions as safety signpost #4.

#4. Draw on Scripture's wisdom for guidelines in your relationships. "Draw boundaries in relationships with the opposite sex. A psychologist says he avoids scheduling a woman for his last appointment. A minister keeps a counselee on the other side of a desk and keeps the drapes open. A doctor calls a nurse into the room when he examines a woman patient. A boss and secretary can avoid going to dinner as a twosome or working evenings alone. A homemaker can avoid tempting situations with neighbors when her husband is out of town. A smart wife won't spend three months at a cottage leaving her husband to fend for himself. Neither will she look after the husband of some other wife who has gone away for the summer. Nor need a husband show undue solicitude for a wife whose husband must be away on business. She needs to feel a gap that only her husband can fill.

"Do such boundaries mean avoiding warm relationships between men and women? Of course not. The Bible gives us the model. Paul advises Timothy to regard 'an elder . . . as a father; and the younger men as brothers; the older women as mothers; the younger as sisters.' You can enjoy warm relationships with the opposite sex. The brother-sister relation includes identification. It expresses concern and shows love. It includes caring and even touching under some circumstances. A warm handclasp can express support. But avoid any physical contact that carries overtones of sexual attraction. What boundaries you set will depend on the amount of electricity. Abstain from all appearance of evil."

Dr. Carlfred B. Broderick sums it up in another way. "If you find yourself in a situation involving delicious privacy with an attractive member of the opposite sex, you should begin to look for ways to restructure the situation." Unless you do this, your foot will be caught in your own net.

In spite of the many pressures that come against modern marriages, a husband and wife can learn from the timeless wisdom of Gen. 2:24: "A man shall leave his father and mother and shall cleave unto his wife." The word "cleave" means "to adhere to, to cling, to hold fast [even in the imagination], to be cemented together."

Charlie and Martha Shedd, whose family seminars share insights gained from many years of happy marriage, reaffirm their commitment to each other in this meaningful prayer:

> *Lord, we commit to you*
> *Our eyes,*
> *Our minds,*
> *Our urges,*
> *And we pledge ourselves*
> *To absolute fidelity.*

Chapter Seven

The If Onlys

"IF ONLY I WERE DIFFERENT!"

FROM the fantasy survey results shared in Chapter 2, and from many other studies of feminine sexuality, we have learned that one out of every three women fantasizes not so much about a different partner as about herself *being different*! For most of these women, the differences fantasized are physical. This was the case for the four women whose letters are quoted from here:

"Whenever my husband and I are in intimate moments, I always imagine that I am more petite, more seductive, more beautiful . . ."

"I must admit that when my husband makes love to me, I am imagining that I am the lovely girl he met during the war instead of the grandmother that I am now!"

"There are many times when I don't want my husband to touch me, not because I don't desire him, but because I am feeling so ugly! I think all wives go through this. In those times I don't push him away, but I picture myself as more desirable, as a pretty Polynesian or a blond beauty queen."

"Several years ago I underwent a radical mastectomy. My

husband is a wonderful man and we have continued to have a wonderful sex life, but I'll be frank in saying that when my husband and I are making love, I always picture myself as I looked at eighteen, instead of the way I look now. Surprisingly, my husband says that *he* does not need to imagine this to feel fulfilled, but I need to see myself as more sensual than I look now."

For a woman to use her imagination in this way is very natural. Some researchers have gone so far as to say that the single most important factor in a woman's sexual fulfillment is that *she feels desirable* and worthy of the attention she is receiving. She must feel lovable. She must feel attractive.

However, problems can arise if a woman begins to use a fantasy image of herself continually, as an escape from reality. Remember the story of Mary Lou? She identified with the attractive heroines of romantic novels so habitually that she avoided the reality of her weight and health problems.

In the world of literature, there are many examples of characters who succumb to this type of fantasizing. Among them is Blanche DuBois in the Tennessee Williams play *A Streetcar Named Desire*. Blanche escapes the unhappiness of middle-aged life by convincing herself that she is a fine young southern lady with dozens of suitors. When confronted with the true circumstances of her existence by an insensitive brother-in-law, she retreats further into her fantasies. In the movie version of *A Streetcar Named Desire,* Marlon Brando gave a memorable portrayal of the brother-in-law, whose seething anger could be summed up in the words, "Wake up, Blanche! You could have a good life!"

Romance in reality does *not* flow from a woman who continually dreams "I am different." In their thorough study, *The Romantic Love Question and Answer Book,* clinical counselors Nathaniel Branden and E. Devers Branden list four aspects a woman must develop if she is to build a romance in reality:

"1. *A woman must develop a healthy level of self-esteem.*

"The individual must see herself as worthy of love." (She must learn to see herself as God sees her: "You are more precious than many gems" (Prov. 31:10).

"2. *One must develop a certain degree of autonomy.*

"She should have her own capacity for self-reliance and self-regulation. She should feel in control of herself, not undisciplined." She cannot be too emotionally dependent, or she will "drain" her partner until he is emotionally dry. She should not expect her lover to meet *all* of her inner needs. She must learn that "out of your innermost being can flow rivers of living water" (John 7:38).

"3. *A woman must develop her own set of values.*

"She needs to know what counts the most, what she cares about, what is important to her, and how she can communicate those feelings." A woman does not need to accept the value system set by advertisers—she must know that she does not have to be as skinny as the model for Calvin Klein jeans to be attractive and desirable! "Do not let the world squeeze you into its mold, but be renewed in your minds" (Rom. 12:2— J. B. Phillips).

"4. *There must be the development of one's own inner resources.*

"This is imperative, so that she is not bowled over by the normal difficulties, obstacles, and frictions of life in general. If a woman has inner resources, she can move through the normal highs and lows of any human relationships." She will discover that others, especially the man who shares her life, are drawn to this inner wholeness. The fruit of the Spirit in our lives is an overflow of "love, joy, peace, patience, kindness, goodness, faithfulness, gentleness, and self control" (Gal. 5:22—NAS).

If these four components are developed, a woman will be able to build a romantic love that is enduring. And if a woman has developed this wholeness of personality, her occasional imaginings that she is *temporarily* different—more attractive, more appealing—are not a real problem. Both the use and the limitations of these fantasies are clear from some responses to the survey:

"We moms do not always have the *time* to look as nice as we would like when our husbands are ready for intimacy. I do not want to push Jim away with the attitude of 'Wait until I'm perfectly ready.' Early in our relationship, I used to imagine myself as having my hair done, etc., just to feel relaxed and receptive. But the most amazing thing has happened in me . . . the more I *focus on Jim* and his needs and desires, the less I think about myself at all—and I am finding *great pleasure and fulfillment*."

Another response to the survey was written with humor and honesty:

"At times we *all* wish we looked better. Men must not care about that as much. Why else do men always seem to prefer the lights on during lovemaking, and gals often prefer the lights off? I for one know I look better in semi-darkness!"

"We have read that tension is one of the greatest killers of sexual feelings. I think the use of my imagination to temporarily think that I look better is a great help to feminine arousal, because then I am less tense. But I have noticed that if I always imagine that I am someone else, then I must be feeling very insecure about my own ability to be sexually exciting."

"This is one area where a mass media society and mass advertising has really hurt women. The gals in the ads and on TV looks so perfect. *Past generations of women didn't have these fantasy women to measure themselves against*."

"IF ONLY MY SITUATION WERE DIFFERENT!"

Besides the fantasy of being different ourselves, we often fantasize about our situation being different. We all have had dreams of fame, fortune, opportunity, or adventure. A full 32 percent of the women who responded to the fantasy survey have most often daydreamed about being in a different situation.

"If only I were wealthy," a young wife wrote. "Well, maybe not wealthy, but just more comfortable than we are now. Then I could afford to dress nicely and belong to a gymnasium, and I would really be happy."

"If only I had a real career," sighed a mother of four grown children. "Then I could overcome my depression."

"If only my life weren't so boring," confided a mother with several young children. "I dream of far-off places and high adventure."

"I dream about being a popular singer," a midwestern housewife shared. "I hear a song and wish I had recorded it and think about becoming famous. Maybe my dreams are dreams of more recognition."

The "if only" desires that we express in our imagination are not necessarily harmful. *Within each of us there is a powerful resource for self-entertainment, healthy escape, and fuller living.* We are not to fear our imagination, thinking that we will lose touch with reality. Rather, *we are to see our imagination as something over which we have control* and which we can channel.

Our fantasies and daydreams can allow us to master our environment in a way that no machine could. We can entertain ourselves, educate ourselves, change ourselves, and enrich our lives in an infinite variety of ways with the resources God has placed in our human soul and spirit. The Bible talks about minds which are in control, which are "under His Lordship." *From the inner resources that God has given each of us, we can actually forge a better reality.*

Daydreaming actually brings the creative right side of your brain into action. Many women have used their imagination to find *solutions to problems,* such as how to move from working in a safe-but-dull bookkeeping job to operating a small boutique which will provide more creative satisfaction.

Other women have used their imaginations to *conquer old habits*. A woman from North Carolina wrote, "I wanted to be a good mother, but I tended to be quick-tempered and easily angered. About a year ago, I began to daydream about how I *should* react in certain situations. How should I react if one of the children accidentally breaks a dish? How should I handle my toddler if he is simply tired and cranky? I can't tell you how much these mental rehearsals are helping my patience and emotional stability as a mother!"

In recent years, the imagination has even been shown to be helpful in dealing with a range of physical ailments, from arthritis to cancer. "If I can get my patients to picture themselves on the other side of chemotherapy, healthy and free of cancer," reports Dr. Steven Gold of Western Carolina Hospital, "then they don't seem to suffer as severely from the chemotherapy side effects."

The "if onlys" are normal and can be very constructive. There is, however, a fine line which is easily crossed. The "if onlys" can become very detrimental if combined with certain destructive feelings.

Two of the most destructive feelings are:

1. *Self-pity,* which is often expressed as depression or in daydreams that show our feelings of alienation from those around us.

2. A *misguided value system,* which is often expressed in fantasies that show discontent and envy.

THE HIDEOUS TRAP OF SELF-PITY

Nothing is more damaging to our personalities and our relationships with others than the plague of self-pity. Nothing keeps us more isolated, more stunted in our emotional growth, than that common human habit of feeling sorry for ourselves. Our daydreams will give no comfort and produce no creative results if they are built on the foundation of "poor me." Yet they often are built on this foundation.

In responding to the survey, one woman wrote: "Sometimes I feel so unappreciated. My husband takes me for granted, and my teenagers think I am their slave. Then I start daydreaming about something happening to me, like a serious illness, and about how they might finally appreciate me if I were gone. . . . Sometimes I even picture my own funeral, with loved ones weeping over me because of their loss. . . ."

Her statement echoes a comment made by Garrison Keillor on "The Prairie Home Companion": "They say so many wonderful things about you at your funeral, too bad I'll miss my own by just a few days!"

Another woman wrote, "My life is so boring that sometimes I can hardly even get out of bed to face another day. On those days I daydream of running away, just leaving my husband and kids and running away and starting completely over."

Why are these two examples such destructive daydreams? It is because they are *fueled by self-pity*.

The presence of self-pity in a daydream can often be detected from the *result* of the daydream, as in the following example:

"I have never gotten over the fact that I didn't get to continue what was a promising tennis career. The things I do now just don't seem important. I'm way too old now, but I still get caught up in daydreams about playing at Wimbledon. When I 'come down' from one of these daydreams, I feel *worse* than ever." The result of daydreams fueled by self-pity is that they make us feel *worse than ever*.

The habit of self-pity is a hideous trap. Often, it is a habit that has been coddled for years and has become deeply ingrained. Self-pity is a crippling disease—a disease the individual has chosen.

Dr. William Backus, founder of the Center for Christian

Psychological Services, teaches often on the power of "self-talk," that is, the power of what you tell yourself. Based on years of counseling experience, he believes that most depression and self-pity flow from three areas of misbelief:

1. A person devalues self.
   "I am totally unappreciated."
2. A person devalues the situation.
   "There is nothing important about the things that I do."
3. A person devalues prospects for the future.
   "My chances for happiness are past. My life can't be adjusted."

In her best-selling book *Passages,* Gail Sheehy, who studied women of all ages, concluded that "women in their thirties can spend their efforts ripping apart all that they built in their twenties." Why do they do this? They have, she says, *"the misconception that life cannot be adjusted."*

Some of the women quoted earlier in this chapter are clearly using their imagination to escape from unhappy situations. They daydream about a life that would rip apart present-day realities. They may be women headed toward the action of ripping apart all they have built.

The truth is that *life requires a series of adjustments* if we are to find ongoing happiness and fulfillment. Every marriage, even the happiest, faces adjustments as the partners mature and change. A career choice usually needs adjustment as the individual develops and ages. Family lifestyles need adjusting as children reach new stages and parents face new challenges. How much better for the women quoted if they could use their creative imaginations to discover *possible adjustments* that would bring happiness to their current lives and the lives of their families, instead of continually daydreaming of escape!

As we make creative adjustments, we are following the wisdom of Proverbs: "A wise woman continues to build up her home, but a foolish one tears [her home] down by her own efforts" (Prov. 14:1). We can use this verse to ask ourselves two important questions: "In what way do my daydreams build up my home?" and "In what way do my daydreams tear down my home?"

Life for every woman is a string of pleasant and unpleasant situations, desirable and undesirable events, fulfillments and disappointments. It is not events in our lives that can poison us, but rather, how we *respond* to those events.

Happiness is a choice. We take giant strides in the direction of happiness when we begin to listen to our self-talk and examine the daydreams that are based on self-pity.

Self-pity is a downward spiral. "The more I feel sorry for myself, the more depressed I become," continued the letter from the woman who daydreamed about her own funeral. "I want my husband and kids to be more appreciative, but I end up driving them further away."

The truth is, at a pity-party there is only room for one. Those around us pull back, and we are left more lonely than ever.

We all fall into the trap from time to time. But do we allow ourselves to dwell on these feelings of self-pity? Do we allow ourselves to paint full-color daydreams from our self-pity?

In Psalm 42, David wrestled with self-pity (and for good reason—violent men were threatening his life). We sense the agony in his words, "My soul is cast down within me."

Then David used the kind of self-talk prescribed by Dr. Backus: "Why art thou cast down, O my soul?" He went on to choose hope over despair:

> "I will *put my hope in God.*
> I will *learn to praise Him and be*
> *thankful.*
> *For He is the* help of my countenance."
> (New American Standard)

A MISGUIDED VALUE SYSTEM

"Lifestyles of the Rich . . ."

Not surprisingly, it is in the area of material possessions that the messages of Madison Avenue most directly conflict with what Christianity values as important. And because we are bombarded by million-dollar campaigns of what we should have and what possessions will make us happy—if only we will go out and buy them—our inner value systems have become terribly confused.

In 1989 the national newspaper *USA Today* published a survey of American daydreams. The aspirations revealed by the survey could be summed up in the phrase "Lifestyles of the Rich and Famous."

A full 45 percent of those surveyed listed their #1 daydream as *"being wealthy."* (People in New England and the Northwest were more likely to fantasize about material wealth than those in the Midwest or the South.) The runners-up in order of frequency were "being smarter," "having a better job or more prominence," and a category called "sentimental reminiscing," or daydreaming about "the good old days." (It is important to note that those surveyed were asked *not* to report on sexual fantasies or daydreams and that, in contrast to the survey done for this book, more men were surveyed than women.)

In addition, researchers found that 10 percent of the individuals listed being a *great athlete* as one of their favorite daydreams, while 9 percent daydreamed about *being famous through the media*. A surprising 8 percent wrote that their daydreams centered on *revenge* or *"getting even."*

In the seventies and eighties, we were called the "me generation." Our society is composed of a large mass of individuals who have been trained, by our media and otherwise, to be greedy, especially for material gain. We have magazines called

Fortune and *Money*. We have television programs like "Lifestyles of the Rich and Famous," that show incredible opulence. We have advertising campaigns that push expensive cars by saying "When you've arrived, let them know it."

After twenty years as a political activist, Abbie Hoffman returned to speak on college campuses before his death. "The apathy I am seeing scares me," he reported on the CBS evening news. "Once when I made strong statements I could get a reaction—one way or the other—but now young people don't respond. 'Believe whatever you want to,' they tell me. 'We just want to make some money.'"

All of this has led to a way of thinking dealt with in a 1986 issue of *Newsweek* magazine, whose cover boldly declared "No Children on Board." The lead article dealt with the growing number of couples in America who are deciding to remain childless. Though some of the couples interviewed had good reasons, the majority had chosen this lifestyle because "We know children take a lot of time and money, and we wouldn't be able to afford the ski weekends or art objects which are so important to us."

Children, we see, aren't high on the list of what the advertising industry presents as important. What is important according to advertisers is what you can afford to wear, what you can afford to drive, and where you can afford to live. Children are not valuable in a media society supported by glittering advertisements (unless, of course, children can be manipulated as a market for toddler designer jeans and overpriced toys).

One woman thought about her daydreams as she filled out her survey. She wrote, "Your fantasy survey helped me to do some deep soul-searching. You see, I don't spend a lot of time in romantic fantasies, but I often dream of having a huge home with a pool and thoroughbred horses, a second home in Hawaii, and great clothes and diamonds and sports cars. After I filled out the survey, I realized I never daydream about something as important as being able to afford to send my children to a *good college*! I'm not really picturing being more prosperous—I'm caught up in daydreaming about *gaudy possessions*. Realizing the *shallowness* of my daydreams has shocked me. I think I have been duped."

In direct conflict with the world's pressure to "get things," the Bible makes it clear that things aren't important—*people are*. "No one, though rich as a king, can ransom his own brother from death. God's forgiveness does not come that way. A human soul is far too precious *to be ransomed by even great earthly wealth*" (Ps. 49:7–8; The Living Bible).

Mady Russell tells of a conversation among a group of young mothers gathered for coffee in Olympia, Washington. One of the women commented, "My fantasy is that my husband and I could be rich enough to quit our jobs and buy a sailboat and live on it in the South Pacific, getting away from all of our troubles to real romance."

Mady responded with a little chuckle. "My friend," she said kindly, "obviously you don't have much sailing experience. Let me tell you how it *really* was when my husband and I stayed on a sailboat in Hawaii. . . .

"You don't have time to look like those gorgeous gals in sailing ads. Your hair gets windblown and matted from spray, and your body burns and peels. The sea is never as smooth as a picture. Most of the time it's pretty rough—and your stomach resents it. When it is calm, your husband isn't saying romantic poetry—he's saying, 'Let's patch the sail. Let's swab the deck. Let's scour the galley.'

"Believe me, Jody, *if you want a sailboat, you can have ours!*"

As comedian Bill Cosby quipped, "*You* have to take care of things. All your precious things can't take care of *you*!"

"Lifestyles of the. . . Famous"

Do you daydream about being a famous movie actress? a world-class athlete? a recording artist? a writer who spins out best-sellers? a scientist who receives a Nobel prize?

These are common themes in the daydreams of youth, dreams of looking forward and of great expectations. Such dreams of "becoming" propel us through life and give us hope for the future.

One survey respondent posed several questions of her own: "I am a busy wife and working mother, but I still have dreams of 'fame' like I did when I was a teenager. Am I in the minority? Am I a grown-up who needs to quit thinking like a kid? After all, we all need recognition."

This woman was absolutely correct—*we all need recognition.* But perhaps we need to think through the *difference* between *the desire for recognition* and *the desire for "fame."*

Recognition is "acknowledgment with appreciation." Fame is "great public reputation and renown." Ours is the first culture ever to have a mass-media orientation. We are so inundated with newspapers and television and radio that an entire generation may have grown up believing that recognition means some kind of local or regional or maybe even national acclaim.

When one thinks about it, it gets almost humorous. One television sports announcer put it this way: "During any given pro game I look out over the faces of the men in the crowd and I believe that a great many of them are in a dream world. I'd bet money that a lot of the fans are fantasizing that they are the famous, talented players down on the field!"

Dr. Jess Palmer of Sacramento, California, says that such fantasies of fame may even contribute to injuries to what he calls "the armchair athletes." "There are lots of us who sit in front of the tube and get really out of shape while we imagine that we are the great athletes we are watching. Then comes a Saturday morning flag football game at the annual picnic, and we injure ourselves seriously because *our body is not where our mind is!*"

Christians are by no means immune to the desire for public recognition. This has been called the age of the electronic church. Gifted church leaders appear on the cover of magazines, in radio interviews, or on television broadcasts. It certainly would be easy to pick up the notion that the effective Christian is the prominent Christian.

One delightful film which deals with this common notion is called *An Ordinary Guy*. In the film, a young man named Mark believes that God has told him that he is going "to be effective in a mighty way." Mark begins to daydream, and his daydreams, as pictured on film, are hilarious. In the first daydream, Mark is a big-time gospel singer, with white buck shoes and a rhinestone-studded outfit, thrilling awestruck fans in a coliseum.

In the next fantasy, he is dressed in an ultraconservative three-piece suit and is telling the congregation he pastors, "I am sorry to see that attendance is down a little bit today." (The camera pans back to show a filled cathedral seating several thousand.)

The third fantasy is a blurb from the CBS evening news: "Missionary Mark has been kidnapped by the Marxist rebels of Bula-Bula for his famous work with the natives of that region."

The film is a hilarious account of how one young person was so caught up in his daydreams of prominence and in the nameless cloud called "souls" that he planned to reach someday, that he forgot the "souls" that were *right on his doorstep!*

Michael and Stormie Omartian picked up this theme in their song "Big Time." In this song, a young musician calls them in the middle of the night and says:

Christian superstars, that is what you are,
If I could just be Big Time . . .
Surely the Lord can see what it would do for Him
If I could just be Big Time.

And many Christian leaders, such as Frankie Shaeffer, are warning about what they call "the selling of the Church." But though many are concerned with what is happening to the image of Christianity, few have realized the drastic effect on the minds and imaginations of *individual* Christians.

What does the Bible say about seeking fame or recognition? "You should think differently than those in the world," Jesus said in Matthew, chapter 20. "Whoever wants to be great in my kingdom must be the servant of all." Jesus "made himself of no reputation, and took upon the form of a servant" (Phil. 2:7). It is one of the great paradoxes of Scripture: we gain by giving up.

There are many very sincere and dedicated believers whose motives for seeking recognition are spiritual in nature. In her response to the survey, one woman put into words the feelings of many: "I truly do want to do great things for the Lord. Then I see an evangelism crusade on television where they talk about the three thousand people that have just come forward during one altar call in South America. What they are doing for God really counts. *It makes what I am doing not seem very important.*"

One answer to these words comes from evangelist Billy Graham. I had the privilege of serving on the media team of his Amsterdam '86 Conference. At this conference over 8,000 pastors and evangelists came together from all over the world to receive training. "I am so touched to be around these men and women," Dr. Graham said with tears in his eyes. "I am embarrassed to even be counted as one of them. I have received the attention, but they are out there doing the real work of the Kingdom. I have received my glory here on earth, but they are going to be receiving glory through all eternity."

Mother Teresa, a true saint of the twentieth century, also gives us a lesson in how to view the accomplishment of effective Christianity. In a 1982 television interview, the Nobel Peace Prize winner was asked about her work in India.

"Your Sisters of Mercy must grow very discouraged," a young reporter commented, "because no matter how many they save, there are multitudes left untouched in the vast population of India."

Mother Teresa's answer was a jewel of godly wisdom. "Oh no," she said. "You see, I do not count as you count. *I count the way God counts.* Not by thousands. By ones. The ones we have touched. . . . *There is no way to describe how greatly God values ONE.*"

What a wonderful understanding of the real value system. There is no way to describe how greatly God values the *one* child He has placed in your home, the *one* husband you live with, the *one* neighbor with whom you share His love. When we learn to value individuals as He does, our lives take on wonderful meaning and purpose.

THE POSITIVE POWER IN THE IF ONLYS

Once we have realized the destructive thinking that may have crept into our daydreams—the self-pity, the improper values, the selfishness or envy—we can begin to walk down a fantastic road of discovery—the discovery of the riches of the imagination God gave us.

"It is my will that you go and bring forth fruit in your lives, the kind of fruit that will be lasting" (John 15:16). Our Heavenly Father does not just want us to have a vivid or fruitful imagination; He wants our imagination to enable us to be *fruitful in reality*.

The creative, imaginative part of our personalities is perhaps the way we are most Godlike. It is true that our imaginations are certainly "fallen," but we were made "in His image," and the Creator allows us to be creative! Theologically speaking, creativity is the image of God in man. God created the world "ex nihilo"—"out of nothing." Like God, in fantasy man creates worlds ex nihilo, out of nothing.

Twentieth-century doctors and scientists are only beginning to grasp the power and benefits that the mind can have on the body. Since the 1960s, many physicians have found biofeedback techniques to be helpful to their patients. Biofeedback is a method of learning to control body functions that ordinarily cannot be regulated voluntarily. People have been taught to regulate their blood flow, body temperature, and even heart rate. This means that biofeedback is helpful in conditions such as high blood pressure and migraine headaches, for our minds can be a powerful tool against tension.

Imagery Helps Us to Reduce Stress

At the beginning of this chapter, a survey respondent was quoted as saying she could not relax and be sexually aroused when she was "feeling ugly."

This woman's tension about her perceived "ugliness" could easily hinder her ability to respond to her husband's advances. The relationship between stress and sexual dysfunction has been pointed out by countless physicians. The body cannot do two things at once; it cannot simultaneously work off stressful feelings and cooperate with sexual arousal.

In her book *The New Sex Therapy*, Dr. Helen Singer Kaplan calls attention to the fact that much sexual dissatisfaction begins when partners pay too much attention to the actual sensations they experience and go about trying to increase those sensations:

> A husband who is concerned about the presence or absence of an erection may find his drive diminishing. A woman who is tense because she is afraid she won't have an orgasm

may be unable to have one. All of this is known as "spectatoring"; the participants seem to stand outside of themselves, judging the way they perform. In this day when sexual "technique" has been stressed, we should remember the effect that our thoughts have on our responses. It is not surprising that "performance anxiety" can be devastating.

In some cases of sexual dysfunction, counselors use imagery to help a couple overcome a mind-set that produces tension. For example, young mothers who no longer seem to desire sex are counseled to block their surroundings out of their minds during lovemaking. Husbands whose sexual appetites have been affected by extreme work pressure are counseled to "picture themselves with their wives in another state, or even another nation"!

There are myriad other situations in which the use of the imagination can relieve stress. And the healthy use of the imagination in times of stress is certainly nothing new.

The familiar poetry of Psalm 23 is for many the highlight of the entire Old Testament. Yet the soothing phrases such as "He maketh me to lie down in green pastures" and "He leadeth me beside the still waters" were probably not written when David was a boy tending sheep in the Judean hills. The words of this great psalm were probably written by a young man under great pressure, a king who was able to *see those green pastures and still waters in his imagination, and to picture his God as the ever-present Good Shepherd.*

A social worker from the Chicago area returned her fantasy survey with a special note:

"The turnover rate for social workers in our area is eighteen months to two years. We see so much child abuse, so much crime, so much heartbreak that most of my co-workers just burn out and turn to other professions.

"Several years ago, though, I discovered the verses in the

book of Revelation about the healing of the earth, verses like the ones which talk about a river that will flow out of the New Jerusalem and heal everything it touches. I discovered other similar verses in the book of Isaiah.

"Whenever I have had a day that makes me want to quit, I have a simple time of prayer, and then I imagine how things will be when the Lord finally returns to set everything right. I believe that learning to use my imagination in this spiritual way has given me the courage to keep on facing what I face every day on the job."

The imagination can also reduce stress by enabling us to envision and face tense situations ahead of time.

For example, if a person who has an extraordinary fear of standing in front of others must make a speech, that person can rehearse the speech mentally. He pictures himself doing well, and not poorly. He pictures the response of the audience as positive, and not negative. He relieves the stress of the actual event by imagined rehearsals.

As mentioned earlier in this chapter, a young mother who responded to the survey used rehearsal in another way: she used her imagination to help her change a habit, the habit of responding with anger toward her young children. How many people could benefit by her example of using daydreams to change bad habits!

A woman from New Mexico sent the following note with her daydreams survey:

"Many precious evenings with my husband had been shattered by my quick tongue, my tendency to speak without thinking. I had always thought, 'I can't help it—this is the way I am.' But *I began to imagine how I should react to my husband,* to have a mental picture of being in control and able to listen to Larry when he was trying to talk to me, instead of saying things that drove him away from me. This may be different from the way most people think that the imagination can help your sex life—but it helped mine! My husband and I are much closer and feel more intimate, and that is what good sex comes from, isn't it?"

Daydreams Help Us to Plan Our Future

Barbara Sher is a counselor based in New York City who specializes in helping women to overcome depression and become more successful. One thing that she has learned to do is to ask women to share their favorite daydream. In a *Ladies' Home Journal* article entitled "When Dreams Come True" (Jan. '85), she stated, "When someone starts off with, 'You're going to think this is silly, but . . . ' then I know that I'm about to be told the *real* dream, the dream that matters to the woman, the one that will make her eyes light up and bring an excited blush to her cheeks." Once she has convinced a woman to not be apologetic for dreaming, Sher goes on to convince her that the desires behind the dream are not always silly or unworthy.

Too often, women act like martyrs in areas of their lives where they do not have to! They throw themselves so wholeheartedly into their roles as wives and mothers and workers that they repress or ignore many of their own gifts. *Our daydreams sometimes stem from gifts or talents that are begging to be allowed to surface.* Examining them can help us to understand ourselves.

The wisdom of Proverbs teaches us, "Many are the plans in a heart, but it is the Lord's purpose that prevails" (19:21). Harriet had the joy of seeing this verse worked out in her own experience.

Harriet was a New York wife and mother who had wanted to be an actress ever since she had a part in her sixth-grade school play. She finally decided to take acting lessons for her own pleasure despite her thought that "it is ridiculous for a woman of forty-five to pursue her childhood dream." Then classes at a local college led to contact with a group of actors who used sign language to present famous plays at schools for deaf children up and down the East Coast. And Harriet had raised a deaf child! Harriet is an actress now, and the kind of acting she does brings more fulfillment than she ever could have imagined.

"I now believe that my nagging desire to take acting classes was a God-given desire," Harriet says. "I love the verse in Philippians, chapter 2, that says 'God is at work within you, giving you desires which are pleasing to Him.'"

Many women have dreams that began in childhood but were later set aside simply because of time pressure and family responsibility.

In order to make creative use of your daydreams you need to do several things. First, examine your dreams. If they are based on self-pity, lay them aside. If their basis is creativity, consider them. Second, reach out for support from those around you. Third, begin to take small steps toward making those dreams come true.

"Do something!" Barbara Sher says emphatically. "Make a short-term plan, start right away. If you want to write, tell yourself that by the end of the week you'll have an outline and at least one paragraph. Better yet, use your most artistic prose to write a letter to someone who needs encouragement today."

Eleanor is a young mother who is experiencing the joy of seeing simple daydreams become reality:

"If my present becomes too oppressive (such as when I am up in the night with sick children), I have learned to let my mind wander over pleasant events of the past and hopeful scenes for the future. In this way, I can eliminate boredom and make realistic plans for the kind of life I will lead when my twins are no longer babies. Last year I realized that I most often think back to special dates and vacations my husband and I had before the children, and that my daydreams for the future included the hope of great family vacations. I realized that I could use this creative energy to plan our vacations way in advance, to find the best deals, to put aside small amounts from the monthly budget. I had been just daydreaming about great vacations because I thought they were impossible with small children. But by moving toward my desires with long-term planning, I find they're coming true!"

"My childhood dream was to become a foreign missionary," wrote a woman from Phoenix. "Both my husband and I were devastated when our application was turned down. Then, my second child was born with several handicaps. I felt like I gave up my dream of being a missionary forever. Then, just a year ago, I began to turn my imagination to ways in which I could be a missionary—one who crosses cultural barriers with the love of God. I began to think of reaching out to the other cultures within our own city. My husband and I are even planning vacation Bible school for a nearby Indian reservation that has requested workers. Why didn't I use this creativity years ago? The inner dream to do some kind of cross-cultural work was from God."

The most often quoted phrase of the late civil rights leader Dr. Martin Luther King, Jr., is "I have a dream."

At the civil rights march on Washington, D.C., in 1963, he went on to define that dream:

> I have a dream that one day this nation will rise up and live out the true meaning of its creed: we hold these truths to be self-evident; that all men are created equal.
>
> I have a dream that one day on the red hills of Georgia, the sons of former slaves and the sons of former slave owners will be able to sit down together at the table of brotherhood.
>
> I have a dream that one day my four little children will live in a land where they will not be judged by the color of their skin, but by the content of their character.

Martin Luther King, Jr., enabled his followers to see the dream which was his own inspiration. How powerful is a dream like this? Powerful enough to inspire the masses, to last for generations, and to begin to change the attitudes of a nation.

It is harmful if we continually must imagine ourselves as different, for then we are not valuing ourselves as God values us. It is not wrong to use our imaginations to relieve tension, as David did so movingly in Psalm 23, for this creativity is a God-given blessing.

It is wrong to wallow in the if onlys of self-pity, of the wrong value system, or of imaginings fueled by pride and envy. It is not wrong to have a vision for the future. The wisdom of Proverbs warns us, "Where there is no vision, the people perish" (29:18).

It is not wrong, however simple or profound our hopes may be, to say . . .

I HAVE A DREAM.

Chapter Eight

The What Ifs

TORMENTING fear that something bad is going to happen to someone you love . . .

Mental pictures about other people which are unfounded delusions . . .

Images of nervous breakdowns or physical illness . . .

Unnamed dread or anxiety . . .

In addition to fantasies that are sensual or erotic and fantasies of fame and fortune, there are other mental images that fight for a place in our imagination. Fantasies that center on unfounded fears, although less common than the other kinds of fantasies, at some time trouble us all.

Jill, in answering the survey, wrote, "During the first year we were married, my husband had to travel many miles on the L.A. freeway to and from his job. Sometimes, if he was extra-late getting home, I would begin to imagine that he had been in a horrible wreck. By the time he did get home, I would be in a terrible, tearful state. He thought that I was a little neurotic, until we talked to some other young couples and found out how many of the wives suffered from these *same* gripping fears."

Leslie wrote, "My husband tells me that I have trouble with my imagination, because I always think that people are down on me. He feels that I am supersensitive to casual glances or remarks. I wish there was a way out of this terrible trap."

In learning that many young brides were dealing with the same gripping fear that she felt, Jill had discovered one of the principles of mental anxiety: most of us face the same things. "There has come upon you no strange affliction." (II Pet. 5:9.) No trial is unique to you.

CERTAIN SEASONS ARE CRUCIAL

There are certain seasons of life in which human beings are more prone to fear than at other times.

Child developmentalists have learned that the first siege of nightmares or horrifying fears usually occurs at about the age of five. This is because the imagination of a child of that age is in full bloom, and because the child has more input and mental stimulation than when he or she was a toddler. Parents of a little one besieged by bad dreams or vivid imaginings need to know that this is a *stage* of development and that *calm reassurance* and *support* are crucial.

There are other fears to be dealt with throughout even the most happy and normal of childhoods—fears accompanying new experiences like spending the night away from home for the first time, the fear of rejection by peers, and concerns about bodily changes in puberty. But by and large, the next most crucial time of dealing with fear is the pulling-up-roots stage of the late teenage years.

The *pulling-up-roots stage* is the point in life where a young person makes efforts to become more independent. It is a necessary and natural phase of human development. This increased autonomy is meant to happen slowly over several years, but it can also happen abruptly with rebellion and turmoil. And in either case the pulling-up-roots stage is a time of emotional vulnerability to fear.

"Do I have what it takes for college?" the young adult asks. "What about a career? Do I have enough brains? enough talents? Am I attractive enough? Will I find someone who really loves me?"

At its highs, this is a time of life filled with anticipation, confidence, and great expectations. At its lows, it is characterized by extreme anxiety and indecision. Unconquered fear at this stage can drive a young person to isolation and withdrawal from others, to dependency on drugs and alcohol, and to conditions like anorexia nervosa.

The next stage of vulnerability tends to come earlier for women than for men. A man in his twenties and early thirties is often in an aggressive "getting ahead" stage. A woman of that age, however, is often *bearing and nurturing small children*. She is the perfect target for fantasies of fear.

Pregnancy unavoidably brings certain fears. There is the natural fear of pain in the coming birth (a fear that's certainly not helped by all of the horror stories we hear from other women!). There is the understandable feeling that "my body will never be the same." Most horrifying of all, there is the nagging worry that "something is wrong with the baby I am carrying."

In 1977, I wrote a book for expectant mothers entitled *The Child Within* (Tyndale House). As that book has continued to be reprinted and distributed, I have been overwhelmed by the responses to the chapter dealing with the fears of pregnancy.

"Besides dealing with the physical fears for my unborn child that women have faced from the beginning of time, I am dealing with the fear of bringing children into a troubled world, into the nuclear age," confided Debbie Boone Ferrar before she gave birth to twins. In an interview in *Good Housekeeping* magazine, Debbie said, "I found great comfort in reading *The Child Within* and knowing that I am not alone in the fears that I'm fighting."

Fears don't end when a child is born. One woman wrote:

"I was terrified during my pregnancy that something would be wrong with our son. Now that he is a toddler, I am afraid that he will be kidnapped from the backyard or something. But someday there will be new thoughts to torment me—he'll go off to school and face drugs. And someday he'll get a driver's license and be out late in the family car. I have just realized that, sooner or later, I'll have to deal with these fears of mothering—I might as well face up to them and find victory now!"

If only every young bride knew that fears of the death of her husband were *not* premonitions, but fears common to young brides! If only every expectant mother knew that other expectant women are being pierced by the thought "Something is wrong with the child I am carrying"!

Another stage of life at which femininity makes us vulnerable to fear occurs when a woman goes through the physical changes known as menopause, generally in the *late forties and early fifties.*

In his book, *What Wives Wish Their Husbands Knew About Women,* Dr. James Dobson deals with the physical, and resulting emotional, changes of midlife. He observes that the feminists have actually hindered the medical and clinical research which was being done in this area. In their determination to see women treated equally in the work place, some feminist leaders insisted that men and women were *not* significantly different physically. In the past four years, however, great strides have once again been made in the understanding of the hormonal changes of midlife.

The fantasy survey and letters received document the idea that women of this age become, once again, more prone to fear. One woman wrote:

"In my thirties and early forties, I was a pretty confident, happy woman. Then, two years ago, I just began to fall apart emotionally. I began to hear the thought 'You are going crazy. You are going to have a total nervous breakdown.' It did not help when a physician suggested I see a psychologist! Finally,

I began to resist those tormenting thoughts, and at my husband's insistence, I searched for a doctor who would really help me. An excellent gynecologist diagnosed very real physical problems, and I am now feeling like a new woman!"

It is a tremendous help to recognize the seasons of a woman's life in which fear tries to raise its ugly head. Later we will see how our unfounded fears can be defeated.

SOME PEOPLE ARE MORE VULNERABLE

Some of us were raised in a way that left us more vulnerable than others to fearful illusions.

In many cases fears stem from horrifying childhood experiences. Emotional scars from these too-real-and-vivid memories must, and can, be healed. Often, when Jesus faced an individual in desperate need, He asked, "Do you *want* to be whole?" What an odd-seeming question! Our first response is usually "Of course I want to be whole!" But do we really? Do we want to be free of fearful memories so badly that we are willing to face them? For, almost without exception, freedom from fearful memories comes from taking the hand of a loving Heavenly Father and, with His help, *facing those fears head-on*.

In many other cases, though, grown men and women face fear as adults, not because of bad childhood experiences, but because they were *overprotected* as children!

The survival of the human race depends on a blending of caution and boldness, with neither being extreme. Many fears are innate, but most fears are learned.

Children learn to fear not only from parents, but from friends, other family members, and even teachers. A fearful adult tends to infect a child with his or her own particular fears. In fact, studies suggest that fear is the most easily transmitted of human emotions.

Our children watch how we respond in life, so our actions

have a greater effect on them than any verbal instructions we give. But, if children are continually cautioned about the dangers of life, instead of being encouraged to face its challenges, they are likely to develop a large number of fears.

The Cinderella Complex, a best-seller by Colette Dowling, addresses women's fear of independence. Ms. Dowling traces many of her adult fears to the fact that she was overprotected as a child, and finds that she is in agreement with the researchers of our time:

> Fearfulness has long been considered a natural component of femininity. The idea of being afraid of the dark, or of being alone—these are things that have been considered ordinary for women, but no longer. Psychologists have now taken the position that phobias, or irrational fears, are no more normal or healthy in women than they are in men.
>
> "Many women's phobias can be traced back to having had overprotective parents," says Dr. Ruth Moulton, "parents who frighten their daughters by laying their own anxiety trips on them. They tell their daughters that they should get home early from dates, that they must watch out for kidnappers, that they can't date new acquaintances. There are reasons, of course, why girls should be wary, but the crippling effects of continual childhood threats and warnings indicate that education in self-defense would be a more constructive course for young women than teaching them that they need to be afraid and watchful if they are going to survive!"

Many researchers think that, in part, women's problems with fear and anxiety stem from insufficient stress when they were young. Psychologists agree that the die of independence is cast before a child reaches the age of six. They now believe that girls may be prevented from taking a certain crucial turn in their emotional development precisely because the way is made too easy for them—because they are overprotected and overhelped and are taught that all they have to do to keep the help coming is be good.

Colette Dowling writes about this connection between over-protection and fear:

> This early indication on the part of mothers—what some researchers call 'apprehensive oversolicitude'—leads children to doubt their own competence. "If Mommy's afraid I can't make it, she must know something I don't," thinks little Debbie.
>
> Coming out of a parent's greater fear for their girl children is the tendency (one might accurately say compulsion) to protect—to jump and catch the baby before she even stumbles, to make sure she doesn't hurt herself. . . . Teaching her daughter to continually avoid risk, the anxious mother inadvertently prevents the child from learning how to deal with fear.
>
> The simple truth is that the only method both humans and animals have for learning to master fear in new situations is to approach and withdraw from a frightening situation repeatedly.

In recent years, Americans turned pitying eyes toward the late Howard Hughes as the irony and sorrow of his last years was revealed. Once the richest man in the world, an inventive genius, a playboy who could afford to have anything and do anything, Hughes spent his last years in lonely paranoia, terrified of imagined germs and illnesses, isolated from the world. Why did this man who could have everything end up enjoying nothing? The answer lies in his biography—an incredibly overprotective mother had paved the way for delusions and mental illness.

Examples like this are especially relevant to the well-meaning mothers of this generation. In our determination to be good and protective parents, will we shield our children so much that we harm them? Will we overhelp our children and hamper their self-confidence?

These are uncomfortable questions, to be sure, but questions that must be considered.

A LIFE OF RESTRICTION

Fear can, of course, be healthy. Healthy fear is what causes a little child to jump away from a loud, unexpected noise. Healthy fear causes us to buckle our seat belts to avoid injury in an automobile. Healthy fear is what allows a young boy to run away from an angry bully twice his size. Fear is a *fuel* that moves us out of dangerous situations and a positive force that can save our lives.

The greatest fear inherent in humans is the *fear of the unknown*; this fear is the basis of many others. When a person, a thing, or an object is unknown, we have no control over it. If we are in control, we feel secure. If we are out of control, we tend to feel insecure.

But, while fear is natural and sometimes healthy, it can also become unhealthy. The Bible says that "in the later days, men's hearts will be failing them because of a host of fears." Fears can multiply and pressure us and restrict our lives. "It is anxiety in the heart which weighs it down" (Prov. 12:25).

A *phobia* is a special kind of fear that is out of proportion to the situation. There are many phobias, each centered on a certain class of objects or events:

Acrophobia—the fear of heights
Claustrophobia—the fear of closed spaces
Hydrophobia—the fear of water
Mysophobia—the fear of dirt or germs
Ophidiaphobia—the fear of snakes
Arachnophobia—the fear of spiders

There is even pedophobia, the fear of children.

One of the most common and constricting of all phobias is

agoraphobia, the fear of open spaces. People with agoraphobia are afraid of being in public places such as shopping malls, buses, theaters, and churches.

Such fear may develop gradually, becoming more and more confining. For example, a woman who travels to work on an express bus may one day feel sudden panic, perhaps even dizziness or loss of breath. Because she could not get off the bus immediately if the panic were to occur again, she begins to take the local bus. When panic occurs there, she begins to get up early to walk to work. Eventually, she limits her walking to her neighborhood, then to her yard, then to her house. It may sound extreme, but many people struggle this way for years. They are prisoners in cells of their own making.

Others deal with timidity, which is less severe.

"I would not say that I am phobic," wrote Janet, "but I sure deal with a fear of standing in front of people. If I am asked to give a report in front of the PTA, or even lead a public prayer for a Bible study, I have horrible mental pictures that I will just stand there, frozen, with my mouth hanging open, or that I will say something that everyone will think is so stupid."

Ungrounded phobias and other fears are being treated more and more by the proper use of the imagination, examples of which were given in Chapter 7.

However, some people are afraid of a number of unrelated objects or events. In these individuals, as soon as one fear is conquered, another crops up. The presence of many and varied fears shows the need for a deeper answer.

Too often, an individual can receive secondary psychological gains from nurturing a phobia. (Once again, remember that Jesus often asked, "Do you *want* to be whole?") For example, a woman who is afraid to drive will have others drive for her. The phobic person often succeeds in manipulating others to his or her own end. But the secondary psychological gains are more than canceled out by the losses: the individual knows inwardly that he or she is manipulative and faces a continual lowering of self-esteem.

Before attempting to clear our imagination of tormenting fear, it is important that we recognize once again the source of that fear.

First of all, the source is not God. *"It is not God who has given you a spirit of fear . . ."* (2 Tim. 1:7). The Living Bible records this verse so beautifully: "The Holy Spirit, God's gift, does not want you to be afraid of people, but to be wise and strong, and to love them and enjoy being with them."

If it is clear that God is not the source of fear, and if we ourselves do not want to harbor ungrounded, tormenting fear, then what is its source?

Delusions can be defined as "misconceptions or lies." We already looked at the words of Jesus in John, chapter 8, where He declares that mankind has a spiritual enemy, "the Father of All Lies."

The source of delusions is not just one's own past experiences. The source of delusions is not just the fearful phrases that were spoken by your mother and father.

We receive a powerful tool of enlightenment when we recognize that many fears are not born in our own minds, but are "fiery darts" aimed at our hearts and minds by the spiritual enemy.

Once we see that there is, indeed, an enemy, we can begin to fight. We can determine, like Paul, to be "in nothing terrified by our adversary." We can begin to raise the shield of faith.

Faith is not something that works automatically. It is not something that works magically. Faith is an activity—a bold partnering with God in determined action.

Carol's Reaction

Whenever I think of how we react to delusions, I remember an event that happened late one night in my sophomore year of college.

Carol, my roommate, was well known in our dormitory for the practical jokes she had played on all the gals throughout the year. A young Texan named Beverly had proven to be especially gullible and had been a frequent target for Carol's pranks.

Finally, Beverly decided that she had had enough. She decided to play a "get even" joke and prepared for it by buying a hideous Wolfman mask.

One evening as Carol stood brushing her teeth at the bathroom sink, the horrible image of Wolfman flashed in the mirror. Luckily, I had had time to see that whatever it was that had entered our bathroom was wearing a pink bathrobe and slippers. But Carol had no warning. All she saw was a vision of terror. What had started out as a practical joke suddenly turned very serious: Carol screamed and took a giant leap away—a leap that sent her through our shower door, which shattered into knifelike pieces.

Beverly ripped off the mask, crying, "Oh, Carol, I'm so sorry—it's only me, Beverly!" Miraculously, Carol suffered only a few minor cuts.

I know for certain that from that night on, Carol gave up most of her practical jokes. She especially never teased another Texan!

I also know that the event became a graphic illustration for me—an illustration of what a delusion of fear can do. Most of our fears are only *masks* with *no substance behind them*. If we react to the fear, though, we can harm ourselves *as surely as if the mask had been real*.

Lenora's Story

In a letter returned with the survey, Lenora told her story:

"Two years ago, my husband and I had to give up our position as Bible translators at an outpost in South America. We did not leave because we were not effective. We did not leave because our tribal people didn't love us. We left because of my fear and anxiety.

"Every time my husband was gone into the jungle for several days to visit other tribes, I would begin to believe that he was not coming back. I would picture a horrible accident or an attack from guerrilla soldiers. I would honestly begin to feel that he had been *killed*. I would begin to fret over the future—how I would get the children home to the States, how I would support them with my husband gone. By the time he arrived back at our station, I was actually surprised to see him.

"The most diabolical thing about my fear is that I guess I thought it was *God's way of forewarning me* about what was going to happen. Because of that, I didn't push the fear away. I became a nervous wreck. Finally, in defeat, we came home.

"I mentally buried my dear husband many times, and *I suffered as much grief and anguish as if I had really lost him*."

DOOM OR DESTINY

Many women who suffer from the fear of what ifs are suffering because they are living out a kind of mystical *Christian fatalism*. Without realizing it, they live as if the events of life are decreed by fate, or doom, or destiny.

As Lenora pointed out, the most diabolical kind of fear is when we are gripped by worry and terror and believe that it is *God* showing us the future.

In the Old Testament, there are some examples of God

giving people warnings about the future. But what kind of warnings were they? And *why* did God send them?

The warnings sent from God were urgings of repentance, warnings that came in love and with an "if" clause. For example, in Exodus the Lord told the children of Israel, "If you keep my ways, I will protect you from a multitude of plagues and diseases. If you abandon my ways, you will suffer the same plagues as the nations all around you." This was not a statement of unavoidable fate: there was an "if" clause.

Other warnings were given to turn people to *prayer and a different course of action,* so that a situation could be *avoided.* God's warnings to Jonah, discussed earlier, are an example. When God spoke through His prophets, it was for a purpose.

Since "God does not give us the spirit of fear," it is imperative that we discover how to *know His voice.* Examples of women involved in this great discovery are given in the next chapter. Understanding His voice and His ways, and rejecting the lies of delusion, is how we begin to battle the what ifs.

The underlying theme of so much fear is the terror of the future, the terror of the unknown. We desire certainty. We want to be assured that we will be all right, that those we love will be all right, that our problems will be worked out, that our questions will be answered.

We cannot know all that will happen in the future, but we can know the One who holds the future. One of the greatest victories in life is to come to the place where we can say, "It is allright for me to not have all of the answers now, or to not know what is going to happen. *God stands with me as I face the unknown.* I will begin to use active faith against the delusions, and to rest in the promises of what God has already said in His word."

Chapter Nine

The Renewed Mind

"Who can set me free from the pattern of my own nature?
I thank God there is a way. . . .
    For He will call her 'beloved' who was not beloved."
                                    —Rom. 9:20, 26; J. B. Phillips

"**I**s there any hope? *Can a person really change?*" The woman on the telephone was calling me cross-country from Roanoke, Virginia. "I have decided I want to *change my thinking patterns*, but I feel like I am locked in a prison of old habits.

"And habits don't change easy with me," the caller continued. "I am the kind who doesn't keep her New Year's resolutions for more than a few days. I have 'turned over a new leaf' so many times that my tree is bare. I have rededicated myself to change so many times that my rededicator has worn out! I don't mean to sound like a pessimist, but I need to know if people can really change!"

This Virginian was not alone in her pessimism.

Clinical counselors admit that many individuals choose to go through extensive counseling and yet remain unaffected by it. "Certainly no patient ever taught me more than the one I call Charlene," writes Dr. M. Scott Peck. "I have had to examine questions such as why she ever entered therapy in the first place, why she persisted in it through some four hundred sessions, and why she totally failed to be affected by it."

Workers at the Shick Centers, a well-known chain that helps people stop smoking, drinking, overeating, and using drugs, have to admit that, though they are proud of their success stories, "some individuals pay the cost of coming through our programs several times, yet remain trapped in addictive behavior."

Dr. Peter Dally, of Westminster Hospital in London, is often called upon to counsel individuals with problems in sexual behavior. In his book *The Fantasy Game,* he writes, "Unfortunately, the results of the treatment are often unpredictable and unsuccessful. As with alcoholics and drug addicts, the outcome of the treatment depends very much on the patient's motivation to be cured. No one abandons willingly and readily something that he feels is needed."

And even the leading humanist philosophers, though dedicated to the ideal that mankind is good and on a path of upward development, must admit that the human mold, when recast, is hardly reformed.

Yet, although change is difficult, there *are*, of course, people who change. People have successfully changed not only their habits, but their personality, and their entire lifestyle.

There is the example of the man now known as Saint Patrick. The son of a prosperous government official in Roman Britain, young Patrick was captured by a group of Irish raiders and sold into slavery in their country. Six years later, Patrick escaped and fled home. He hated Ireland with burning zeal and vowed that he would never return. But while in Britain, Patrick became a Christian. "My heart is entirely new, entirely changed," he told his bishop. Knowing the language of the Irish peoples, he felt compelled to return to the land of his captivity in the year A.D. 430.

Patrick was so *changed* that he is credited with winning an entire nation to the faith. Unlike much of the rest of Europe, Ireland converted without bloodshed—early Christian Ireland produced dozens of saints but not a single martyr. The former slave boy began one of the greatest evangelizing feats in history.

In our own century someone who changed greatly was Malcolm Muggeridge, poet laureate of England. Formerly an outspoken cynic and critic of Christianity, he says, "I came face to face with the love of God while witnessing the work of the Sisters of Charity in India. The undeniable power in that love apprehended me and changed me, revolutionizing my mind and soul." Muggeridge's story can be studied in the books *Malcolm Muggeridge: A Life*, by Ian Hunter, and *Like It Was— The Diaries of Malcolm Muggeridge*.

In an earlier century, another Englishman, John Newton, was captain of one of the most profitable ships involved in the slave trade. After many years as a slave trader, Newton wrote in his diary, "I was a prisoner to every vile habit imaginable. My mind was tormented and uncontrolled."

John Newton was a hardened atheist, but he had an amazing conversion to the Christian faith. He became a major voice in England for the abolition of the slave trade; he testified before Parliament and tirelessly printed and distributed articles about the evils he personally had witnessed. He left the answer to his changed life in a simple but enduring musical testimony, the moving hymn "Amazing Grace":

> *Amazing Grace, how sweet the sound,*
> *That saved a wretch like me.*
> *I once was lost, but now am found,*
> *Was blind, but now I see.*

Saint Patrick, Malcolm Muggeridge, John Newton, were men who were changed. They discovered that the key which released them to change was grace—the grace of God.

"NOT IN MY DICTIONARY"

"Grace" is a term that has gone out of modern usage, and out of the common man's dictionary. "I had heard the word," says Chuck Colson (who was convicted for crimes related to the Watergate scandal and who now heads Prison Fellowships International). "But I could not have defined it. 'Grace' was not in my mental dictionary."

Grace is first of all defined as *"the unmerited, unearned favor of God."* Jesus came to teach us many things, but among all of the amazing things He said, is there anything more amazing than this? No matter where we have wandered, what we have done, God loves us. Grace is the unearned love of the Father toward his child.

The more we understand about His forgiveness and grace in our personal lives, the more we can bring divine grace into our human relationships, into romance. Grace allows us to let down walls of self-defense and barriers of self-protection. We learn to extend grace to others, to convey that "if you have memories which distress you, fear about some awful part of you, you can tell me these things if you like. I will only love you better, because I will know you better." Grace enables us to know, and to be known.

But God's grace is much more than God's unearned favor. It can also be defined as *"the operational power of God."*

In the Gospel of John, chapter eight, we read about a woman who was caught in an immoral act and brought to Jesus to be stoned. Jesus demolished the accusations against her by saying, "He that is without sin, let him cast the first stone." When the woman's accusers walked away in defeat, Jesus said, "Neither do I condemn thee, go and sin no more."

There are only two ways to look at that statement. Unless He was setting her an impossible task, He was telling her that change was possible.

He was offering her forgiveness that would cover her past and grace that would revolutionize her future.

Jesus did not come to earth to show us how to live and then pat us on the back and say "Good luck!" He came, rather, to offer the possibility of change through the *power of His grace,* change through the *presence of His spirit,* and change through the *dynamic of forgiveness.*

NO ONE BATS 1.000!

A great amount of modern philosophy and pseudoreligion tells the individual, "You are not guilty." How can one be guilty if there is no longer such a thing as "wrong"? The situational ethics of the last two decades have asserted that there are no absolutes, that morality changes according to each situation. So . . .

- there is no such thing as embezzlement—only "juggling the books."
- there is no such thing as tax fraud—only "creative financing."
- there is no such thing as military deception—only "covert action."
- there is no such thing as marital infidelity—only "open marriage."

Comedian Robin Williams has poked fun at the self-righteousness of me-ism. He helps us to laugh at ourselves by showing us how thoughts are expressed differently, depending on whether they are in the first, second, or third person.

First person: "I am nicely rounded."
Second person: "You are overweight."
Third person: "She is fat!"

First person: "I am firm in my convictions."
Second person: "You are rather close-minded."
Third person: "He is stubborn and pigheaded!"

First person: "I have a good self-image."
Second person: "You are conceited."
Third person: "He is proud and arrogant!"

These examples are humorous, but our day-to-day expressions of blamelessness are not. Dr. William Glasser says, "I am amazed at the counselees who have come to me believing that they were in no way responsible for their actions or the situation in which they find themselves."

Dr. Glasser has been credited with helping to change the approach of a new generation of therapists. In his best-seller *Reality Therapy,* Dr. Glasser laments the low success rate of Freudian-based approaches. Such approaches view an individual's condition as the result of his or her past and the individual as therefore "not guilty." Glasser's "reality therapy" has been used with great success in state hospitals, juvenile homes, and private practice. It is built on a different but simple premise: "the counselee is himself seen accountable for much of his problem. . . . unless an individual is willing to confront and judge his own behavior, he will not change."

Jesus did not tell His followers, "You are not guilty." He warned that those who thought they had not sinned were in grave danger. Instead of saying, "You are guiltless," He said, "You can be forgiven."

Call it the subconscious or call it the spirit of man; deep within we carry the knowledge of our guilt, the knowledge that "all have sinned and come short of the glory of God," the knowledge that we have "missed the target" in our actions and in our attitudes. Oh, it is true that many others are worse than we are. Our efforts at righteousness are like batting averages in baseball; some bat .250, some bat .300, but no one bats 1.000.

We can contend that our thought-life and fantasies are "better than some other people's," or we can admit to areas that are out of control, based on deception, and tinted with darkness.

Guilt is a heavy weight to bear.

Physicians have linked subconscious feelings like guilt to all manner of physical ailments, from high blood pressure to migraines to stomach ulcers.

And in the emotional realm, a guilty conscience steals the joy from life and closes us off from human relationships. "I do not like the person I have become," wrote one woman in response to the survey. "I can hardly live with myself—how can I expect my husband to keep on living with me?"

If we are locked in a heavy though invisible yoke of guilt, who can turn the key that will release us?

THE DYNAMIC OF FORGIVENESS

Throughout the Old and New Testaments, the Creator continually tells us, "Call on Me, and I will answer you, and show you great and mighty things . . ." (Jer. 33:3). He tells us that there is a storehouse of forgiveness that is ours for the asking!

" 'Though you have scorned my ways from earliest times, yet you still may return to Me,' says the Lord of hosts. 'Come and I will forgive you. . . . And I will open up the windows of heaven for you and pour out a blessing so great you won't even have room enough to take it in' " (Mal. 3:7,10).

Chris Blevins had been a guru of the highest order, seeking for years to climb a spiritual ladder to oneness with God and His universe. When he heard about forgiveness he thought, "Could it be that profoundly clear? I had been trying to empty myself, to become a holy man by my own efforts. But the Bible doesn't say 'be empty.' It says 'be filled with the spirit of God.' "

Blevins was overwhelmed by the promise that "God will

cleanse your hearts and minds through Christ Jesus." "Other religions offer penance and self-denial—I had done more than my share of that," he said. "Only Christianity offers cleansing, and the opportunity for the wall between a man and God to be broken down."

Prayers for forgiveness and grace can take many forms.

In Martin Luther's Small Catechism, we read:

THE GENERAL CONFESSION

Almighty God and Merciful Father, I, a poor, miserable sinner, confess to Thee all my sins and iniquities with which I have offended Thee, and justly deserve Thy temporal and eternal punishment. But I am heartily sorry for them, and sincerely repent of them, and I pray Thee for the sake of Thy boundless mercy, and for the sake of the innocent death of Thy Beloved Son Jesus Christ, to be gracious and merciful to me, a poor sinful being.

For we know from the Scriptures that "He that covereth his sins shall not prosper, but he that confesseth and forsaketh them shall have mercy."—Prov. 28:13

I accept this forgiveness by believing the Gospel.

In the catechism, Martin Luther went on to write, "Every believer can and should be certain of the forgiveness of his sins and of his salvation, because God's promise is sure. This distinguishes the Christian religion from all false religions, all of which teach salvation by works instead of by faith" (#193 of The Apostles' Creed).

The thief who hung on the cross beside Jesus did not have time for a lengthy prayer. He simply but effectively prayed, "Lord, be merciful to me, a sinner" (Luke 18:13).

You may want to be very specific in your prayer, especially since we are dealing here with thoughts and emotions. The psalmist wrote, "O Lord, you have examined my heart and know everything about me. You know when I sit or stand. . . . You know my every thought" (Ps. 139:1–2). He knows you; don't hesitate to pray honestly, without embarrassment. You may want to conclude your specific prayer with the words of Psalm 51:

> *Wash me, and I shall be whiter than snow,*
> *Create in me a new, clean heart, O God,*
> *filled with clean thoughts and right desires,*
> *Cast me not away from Your presence,*
> *and don't take away Your Holy Spirit!*
> *Please give me the joy of Your Salvation.*

"Love to pray," says Mother Teresa. "I often must seek cleansing from the filth and horribleness that I must walk through. But love to pray. An intense inner spirit life is there for us for the gathering, and no limits are set."

CONVICTION VERSUS CONDEMNATION

A great many believers have prayed the forgiveness prayer but still do not receive the full benefits of forgiveness. They do not live life convinced of God's love and mercy. Why?

Because of the heaviness of condemnation.

Forgiveness is more than a one-time event. We can walk in forgiveness. But to do that, we must learn the difference between conviction and condemnation.

Conviction is a work of the Holy Spirit. The Spirit touches our hearts and points out flaws or problems for our benefit, with the purpose of drawing us to God. The Spirit offers instruction and correction, always under a canopy of love. "If we freely admit our need, we find God utterly reliable—He forgives us and makes us totally clean" (1 John 1:9; J. B. Phillips).

Condemnation is different. Condemnation is the destructive work of the destroyer. Instead of turning to God, we are driven away from God. Instead of being built up, we are beaten down.

An amazing picture of condemnation and its source is found in Zechariah, chapter 3, verses 1–6. In a vision, the Lord showed Zechariah a scene in which Joshua, the High Priest of Israel and its "holiest" representative, stood before the Lord.

"Joshua stood before the Angel of the Lord, and Satan was there, too, at the Angel's right hand, accusing Joshua of many things.

"And the Lord said to Satan, 'I reject your accusations, Satan; yes I, the Lord, for I have decided to be merciful to my People—I rebuke you. Joshua is like a burning stick pulled out of the fire.'

"Now Joshua's clothing was filthy as he stood before the Angel of the Lord.

"And the Angel said to the others standing there, 'Remove his filthy clothing.' And turning to Joshua, the Angel said, 'See, I have taken away your uncleanness and sins, and now I am giving you these fine new garments.'"

You can live before God like a woman still clothed in the tattered rags of your own rightness, or you can understand that you have been given a glorious, though invisible, designer gown, a gown already paid for by God's grace.

THE SCHEMES OF THE ENEMY

The most crucial factor in a life free of condemnation is realizing that you, like Joshua, have a spiritual enemy.

In his masterful book *People of the Lie,* Dr. M. Scott Peck deals with the dilemma of human evil and its source. A prominent psychiatrist, Dr. Peck chaired the committee that looked into the psychological causes of Viet Nam's notorious My Lai massacre. Dr. Peck writes:

> In common with 99 percent of psychiatrists and the majority of clergy, I did not think that the devil existed. Having come over the years to the belief in a benign spirit,

or God, and a belief in the reality of human evil, I was left facing the next intellectual question, "Is there a devil?" We were all surprised at how long we have ignored the obvious answer —yes.

The list of intellectuals who have come to believe in an evil spirit could go on ad infinitum, but their opinions could still be shrugged off as "their opinions." The important, inescapable fact is that Jesus believed in a spiritual enemy.

Jesus warned that this enemy is a thief, and said that Satan's work is to "steal, kill, and destroy" (John 10:10). One of the first things that the enemy wants to steal from a believer is the assurance of God's love and the joy of forgiveness. In the Gospel of John, chapter 8, verse 44, Jesus tells how Satan does this: "He [the devil] was a murderer from the beginning of time and a hater of truth—there is not an iota of truth in him. When he lies, it is perfectly normal, for he is The Father of Lies."

The Father of Lies. Lies of condemnation. Lies that bring depression and hopelessness. Lies that cause worry or fear. Lies against God and against those around you. Lies that lead to confusion and delusion and sexual temptation.

"INCORRECT INPUT"

The Apostle Paul warns that believers are "not to be ignorant of the schemes of the adversary." The trouble is that many of us are appallingly ignorant of his schemes! And that means we are pitifully *vulnerable to his lies.*

These lies are hurled at us in several ways. First and most common, there is what the Bible calls "fiery darts" (Eph. 6:18). The Greek word used here is *noema.* Vine's Greek dictionary defines this as a "partial thought," or incorrect thinking.

We must begin to monitor the thoughts that flit across our mental computer screen. So much that is being fed into our mental storage bank should be rejected the moment it is received, the moment we recognize it is an untruth or a partial truth whose source is hellish.

Second, lies whose source is our spiritual enemy can come to us through the words of those around us. When Jesus told the disciples that He was going to be killed but would be resurrected on the third day, Simon Peter cried out, "No, Jesus, this is not going to happen to you!" How surprised he must have been by the Lord's reply! Jesus said, "Get thee behind me, Satan!"

Was Jesus saying that Peter was "possessed"? No. He was recognizing that Peter had given voice to a thought that had been inspired by his spiritual enemy, the devil.

Too often, men and women give voice to lies that are sourced in the evil kingdom. "You are a failure," a little child can be told. Or, "You are so stupid." Or, "You are headed for trouble." The vulnerable child receives that lie as truth and can suffer the consequences for a lifetime.

Adults are certainly not immune to the effects of statements that are negative or condemning.

"You don't look well. You must be really sick," a co-worker says—and we go home and worry ourselves sick.

"How can you say you are going to change?" a mate may ask sarcastically. "Haven't you tried to change before?" We can receive these condemning words like a whip and begin to beat ourselves unmercifully.

A third group of lies are those which come flying at us through our senses. Through the television or movies. Through books we choose or advertisements that grab our attention. Through songs that we hear and sing to ourselves. Through the mass media deluge discussed in this book.

STOP *at this point in your reading. Take a moment to reread the paragraphs above. The concepts they discuss are crucial to the rest of this book, and to your mental and emotional well-being.*

Three sources of inspiration have woven themselves into our

creativity, whether we are creating songs or books or stories or simply daydreaming. The three sources of inspiration are:

Human
Heavenly
Hellish

(A particular inspiration may come from more than one source. So often, input we receive can be partially good but laced with a bit of the poison of untruth, like the chocolate that is swirled into the middle of a marble cake.)

What is the source of condemnation, of the thoughts that drive you further from God instead of drawing you to Him? It is hellish. What is the source of the fiery dart of discouragement that says, "You cannot change, either in thought-life or in lifestyle"? It is hellish.

The truth is that Jesus came to offer change. The woman from Virginia who is quoted at the beginning of this chapter said, "I feel like I am locked in a prison of old habits." Jesus said, "I have come to set captives free."

You can learn to hear God's voice instead of the lies of condemnation, learn to understand when thoughts are inspired by His Spirit. In John, chapter 10, Jesus promised that His sheep would be able to know His voice.

THE RENEWING OF YOUR MIND

Forgiveness is not a one-time experience. We must learn to walk in forgiveness. It is the dynamic of forgiveness, the energizing love of God, that enables us to find the reality of Rom. 12:1–2 (J. B. Phillips):

"With eyes wide open to the mercies of God, I beg you to present your entire being to Him. . . .

"Don't let the world around you squeeze you into its own mold, but let God re-mold your minds from within."

His Spirit delights in helping you change. . . . "He calls you Beloved." And, as we saw in Chapter 3, the need to feel cherished and loved is the deepest need of the human heart.

Chapter Ten

The Fortress of
Your Mind

"A person without self-control is as defenseless as a city
with the outer walls of protection broken down."

—Prov. 25:28

"The person with self-control is more mighty than he who
conquers a city."

—Prov. 16:32

THE following story provides a
humorous illustration of human nature:

A sincere member of his congregation pulled the pastor aside
one morning and pleaded, "Help me, Pastor. Overeating is a
real problem for me. Pray a prayer of deliverance over me.
Cast out the spirit of gluttony."

"My dear," the pastor answered with a twinkle in his eye,
remembering the words of Jesus, "this kind cometh out only
by prayer and fasting . . . *your* prayer and fasting!"

The wise counselor knew the woman was after a quick-and-
easy solution to her problem, instead of the lasting solution:
self-control.

Go ahead—groan out loud! You knew that, sooner or later, we would have to deal with the sticky subject of *self-control*.

In previous chapters, we have looked at ways of thinking that produce a mind "out of control." We have seen that our mind is the target of much spiritual warfare and that we are asked to "cast down vain imaginations" (2 Cor. 10:5), whether those imaginations are fearful, or lustful, or filled with envy and discontent.

We have seen that our Heavenly Father loves us and is willing to invade the darkness which has crept into our lives with His light. In the last chapter, we looked at the dynamic of forgiveness. If we are willing, the dynamic of forgiveness extends to our past, even to the cleansing of the subconscious, and we find ourselves in the same position as the man Jesus mentioned in Matthew, chapter 12—his house (his soul) swept and clean. Because of the dynamic of forgiveness, we have the joy of discovering that "old things have passed away" (2 Cor. 5:17). Jesus warned that the house that was cleaned should not be left empty, but should be filled.

The message of the gospel is not just one of "getting free" from old habits and thought patterns; it is a message of *staying free,* of *living free*. "Now that you know that Christ came to set you free," Paul wrote to the men and women in Galatia, "don't become entangled again with any weight of bondage. Having gained freedom, make certain you stay free."

The initial step of getting free is itself not easy. In response to the fantasy survey, Ricki wrote:

"I had often heard the verse 'The spirit is willing, but the flesh is weak.' 'Boy, that's ME,' I thought, and I flippantly used it as an excuse for a thought-life that was totally out of control.

"But one day I read an Old Testament verse that shocked me. It says that there are people 'whose god is their own fleshly appetites.' In other words, when there are areas of my life I have given into for so long that they rule over me, those areas become a *god* to me. I am actually bowing down and worshiping the god of food, or the god of sex, etc.

"What can we do when our 'flesh' is so weak?"

THE WALLS IN DESTRUCTION

In ancient times, the term "walls of a city" was synonymous with *self-defense*. The walls of protection that surrounded Babylon, for example, were so thick that chariots could race on top of them! The walls of Solomonic Jerusalem were also massive barriers of defense.

The year 606 B.C. brought the darkest days of Old Testament history. Babylon, the ruling power of the world under the leadership of King Nebuchadnezzar, swept into Jerusalem. Homes were looted and burned, Solomon's glorious temple was destroyed, and the people of Zion were led away to slavery. As to the walls of protection which had surrounded that proud city, they were demolished so completely that "not one stone was left upon another." There are stirring archaeological records of this tragedy.

In the midst of this destruction, God spoke through the prophet Jeremiah, promising that after seventy years, the children of Israel would "return with singing unto Zion." Deliverance came exactly as God had promised. In the year 536 B.C., the exiles (some 50,000 of them) were miraculously allowed to return home.

Under the leadership of Zechariah and Haggai, the Israelites set to work to rebuild their homes and their temple. But after almost ninety years of resettling, the people of the city were still vulnerable to attack. Why? The outer walls of their city still lay in ruin.

Thieves and cutthroats could enter the city at will. Mercenaries and foreign troops could plunder the city with ease.

There was no peace or confidence in the lives of those to whom Jerusalem was home.

No wonder Proverbs compares self-control to walls of protection. *Without self-control, we are defenseless.*

And when the walls of self-control are down through years of neglect, can they ever be rebuilt?

How do you rate yourself in the area of mental self-control? Are you well disciplined? Are you disgustingly undisciplined, with walls that are a hopeless "rubble"? Or, like most of us, are you out of control, then in control, then disappointingly out of control again?

HOPE FROM A HISTORY LESSON

Nehemiah is a book of the Old Testament that is seldom read and seemingly unimportant to twentieth-century life. Yet to the individual determined to regain self-control and willpower, the book of Nehemiah is extremely significant and filled with hope. It is the story of the rebuilding of the walls of Jerusalem. It is a handbook for the rebuilding of self-control.

Nehemiah was a Jew who had remained in Babylon as the consultant, or cupbearer, to the new Persian ruler, Artaxerxes. In 446 B.C., Nehemiah received a tragic report from his relatives back in Jerusalem: "The survivors are in great distress and reproach. The walls of Jerusalem are broken down, and its gates are burned with fire."

Without self-control, we are the object of reproach, of criticism. We grow critical and angry at ourselves. "Why," one survey respondent asked, "are my mind and emotions so vulnerable, even after becoming a believer?"

God does not leave us alone, with only our own resources. To Jerusalem, He sent Nehemiah. To us, God sends His Spirit.

The very name Nehemiah means "the consolation of God," or "the consoling breath or spirit of God." In the New Testament, Jesus said to His disciples, "The Comforter is the

Holy Spirit, Whom the Father will send in my Name. He
will teach you all things, and remind you of all that I have
said" (John 14:26; The Living Bible).

It is exciting, then, to view the book of Nehemiah as both
a historical document and an allegory of the walls of our personalities being rebuilt under the leadership and direction of
the Holy Spirit.

When Nehemiah learned that his brothers in Jerusalem were
a reproach among the nations because of their helplessness, he
wept for them and spent many days in fasting and prayer.
Another New Testament name for the Spirit is the *Intercessor*—
the *Mediator* between you and God. He helps our weaknesses,
because He makes intercession for us according to the will of
God (Romans 8:26).

Next, Nehemiah obtained the necessary building materials
from the vast storehouse of the king. Not only were the res-
idents of Jerusalem lacking in hope; on their own they did not
even have the building blocks to restore the walls of self-
defense. When Nehemiah arrived to head the reconstruction,
he brought with him all that was necessary for the completion
of his task.

Nehemiah had something else in his possession. He had
been given letters of authority from the king, the legal clout
to accomplish his plans. He knew that Jerusalem was at the
mercy of an evil warlord, Sanballat. After years of surrendering
the control of our minds and emotions to the attacks of noema
(see p. 173), we find the authority of our own will inoperative.
But the Holy Spirit has the authority of the Creator to work
a new creation.

When Nehemiah first arrived in Jerusalem, the inhabitants
were reluctant to let hope rise in their hearts. They said, "Our
strength is decayed, and there is too much rubbish for us to
even begin" (4:10). Nehemiah began to do what the Holy
Spirit is sent to do in the lives of believers—he taught the
people to pray. In fact, he led them in their prayer, once again

fulfilling his role as intercessor. And as the people learned the discipline of prayer, hope began to rise.

The rebuilding of Jerusalem's walls of protection was not accomplished in a day. Week after week, month after month, Nehemiah led the Israelites in their reconstruction. Against the ridicule of enemies, against the discouragement from within, Nehemiah pressed on. How graphic a picture of the Spirit who is determined to complete all that He has begun in your life!

When "No" Is "Yes"!

To complete his task, Nehemiah had to continually say "no" to the opposition. Our opposition comes in the form of noema—the fiery darts, the erroneous thinking that wounds our hearts and minds. Nehemiah's opposition came in the form of two destructive villains, Sanballat and Tobiah: "When Sanballat the Horonite and Tobiah the Ammonite official heard of it, they were deeply disturbed that one had come to seek the well-being of the children of Israel" (Neh. 2:9–10).

Tobiah was a member of the Ammonites, a hostile tribe that surrounded Jerusalem. Sanballat was the provincial governor of Judah, a spiteful, greedy ruler whose control had been absolute until Nehemiah arrived on the scene. Sanballat's only interest was to keep the people in defeat and despair, captive in his evil dominion.

Yet Nehemiah was able to deal effectively with the obstacles to the restoration. For those rebuilding their walls of self-control, it is extremely important to see how he did it, for *"all these things that happened to them {the Old Testament believers} are object lessons to us; they were written down so that we could read about them and learn from them in these last days"* (1 Cor. 10:11; The Living Bible).

THE STRATEGY FOR CONSTRUCTION

From Nehemiah's actions we see that there are several parts to the strategy for construction.

1. Nehemiah knew that he could not compromise, or negotiate, with his enemy. (Saying "no" to the enemy means saying "yes" to God's plan.)

In Nehemiah chapter six, Sanballat sent a message to Nehemiah. "Come down from your work on the wall," he urged four different times. "Meet me in one of the villages and we will negotiate an agreement." Nehemiah had the wisdom to see that it was a plot, that Sanballat planned to kidnap him and slay him. He knew better than to negotiate with an enemy whose motive was destruction. This, then, was Nehemiah's answer:

"No, I won't stop working on the wall. I am doing a great work, an important work, so that I cannot come down" (see verse 3).

In your life, the attempts to overthrow your self-control may sound something like this: "You have been working so hard on this area. Ease up a little; you're being too hard on yourself."

The reconstructive work going on in your life is an important work. The development of greater self-control is crucial to your own mental health and happiness, and to the happiness of your family and all of those around you. Don't be tricked into compromises.

Belinda's letter underscores the importance of not compromising:

"I have spent a lot of time retreating into a dream world and avoiding reality, but I am determined to regain self-control in this area. I am the kind of person who will have to be very vigilant. You see, I am a diabetic, and there are times when I tell myself I can 'cheat' just a little bit on my diet. In just a couple days, I find myself eating everything in sight! Finally,

I make myself so sick and miserable that I must return to my strict diet. If I give myself an inch, I lose a mile!"

What Are Your "Allergies"?

An allergy is defined as an overly sensitive reaction to a particular substance. An individual can develop this oversensitivity to anything, from cats to pollen to her own hair!

Those of us who have experienced severe allergic reactions know that there is really only one answer—absolute avoidance! Not everyone has to walk a mile to avoid a cat, but I do. My system simply cannot handle feline input.

In the same way, there are some kinds of input to which each of us is "allergic," or overly sensitive. If a woman tends to be melancholic or morose, she probably needs to avoid the input of tearjerkers. If she is vulnerable to fear, why should she read murder mysteries?

Each one of us has areas of sensitivity that we cannot compromise if we want to maintain self-control.

2. Nehemiah wisely rejected the lies of his enemy.
Sanballat tried another lie: he attacked Nehemiah's motives. He said, "You are only doing this for selfish gain."

Too often, the fiery darts that we receive are aimed at God Himself! "After all," you may have heard, "can I really trust my life to God? Does He really care about my well-being, or am I just a pawn in some giant scheme?" Sanballat wanted to discredit the actions of the Comforter sent by the King.

Nehemiah's answer in this instance was "I am not doing this work for selfish reasons. The enemy has invented this idea" (6:8).

How can we answer the enemy when he questions the goodness of God's plan for our life? We use the talk-back technique. We speak the truth:

"I know the plans that I have for you, says the Lord, plans

for good and not for evil, to give you a future and a hope" (Jer. 29:11).

This was the way in which Jesus handled His own great time of temptation. When Lucifer appeared and said, "If you are the Son of God, turn this stone into a loaf of bread," Jesus overcame this scheme and His own flesh by quoting the truth, "It is written that man cannot live by bread alone, but by the Word of God."

3. Nehemiah worked with "spear in hand."

As the protective walls around Jerusalem began to rise, Nehemiah discovered that enemy troops planned to infiltrate the city at night between the remaining gaps in the walls. Nehemiah's plan?

"From that time forth . . . they who built on the wall, and they who bore the burdens, everyone with one of his hands worked on the wall, and with the other hand held a *weapon*. And as for the builders, everyone had his sword girded by his side" (4:17, 18).

In one hand we hold a tool for building, and in the other a weapon for fighting. If God's reconstructive work in our lives is to be complete, we cannot lay down our sword. Ephesians, chapter 5, clearly teaches that the "sword is the word of God." The sword of the spirit is the word of God.

When studied in the original Greek, 2 Cor. 10:5 gives a very practical tool for self-control:

"Casting down imaginations, and every vain thing that exalts itself against the knowledge of God, and bringing into captivity every thought to the obedience of Christ."

The phrase "bringing into captivity" is translated from the Greek word *aichmalotizo*. In New Testament days, this literally meant *"to capture by bringing to sword point."* (When a policeman arrests a suspect today, he points a gun and says, "Hands up!" In Roman times, an individual was arrested when a soldier

brought the tip of his sword to rest against the suspect's heart.)
To early believers, the verse was a clear picture of how we are
to control our thought-life: we expose the thoughts to the
truth of the sharpest of swords—the word of God.

We learn to control lies and delusions by bringing them to
sword point!

Your Untapped Resource

Let's be honest. It is hard to learn to use Scripture as your
spiritual weapon if you have little or no scriptural knowledge.

One woman who answered the survey wrote:

"I have recently discovered that there are dozens of Bible
verses that apply to my mental health, dozens of others that
apply to peace and freedom from fear. I feel cheated, because
I was raised with little or no Bible knowledge. A year ago, I
could not have told you the difference between Noah and
Moses. My folks wanted me to choose what I wanted to believe
when I grew up. So I grew up believing nothing—with a
great moral void. I am doing a lot of digging in the Bible
now to find verses that apply to my own particular needs. . . .
I have a lot of catching up to do!"

She is certainly not alone in her lack of spiritual understanding. Studies have shown that the majority of men and women
today, even those who attend church on a regular basis, have
very little personal knowledge of the Bible.

How can we hope to defend ourselves in a desperate spiritual
battle if we cannot lift the sword?

Doctors William Backus and Marie Chapian have effectively
used "misbelief therapy," which has three basic steps:

1. Locate and identify an error in your thought-life or self-
talk.
2. Argue against that untruth.
3. Replace the error with the truth (as Jesus did in His
time of temptation).

The truth to replace the error can be discovered in God's word.

Here is an example of the three-step procedure:

1. (Identify) "I'm a failure because I am not the perfect wife and mother I wanted to be, and my marriage isn't perfect, either . . ."

2. (Argue back) "I am not a failure just because I don't feel like supermom. My marriage isn't all I want it to be yet, but it has its good points . . ."

3. (Replace) The sword of truth: "We can be very confident of this; He who has begun a good work in us will go on developing it" (Phil. 1:6).

If your ability to use the sword in this way is limited, you can begin today to build up your scriptural arsenal. The daily study of even a short passage of Scripture, the memorizing of even a few verses, can be the beginning of a great metamorphosis in your personality.

There are many modern-language versions of the Bible to help us in our understanding. The Revised Standard Version, the New American Bible, the King James Version, the Living Bible, the J. B. Phillips New Testament, the Amplified Bible—all are excellent choices.

At any interdenominational Bible bookstore, there is also a wide variety of Bible study aids. For memorization purposes the best material probably is still the small verse packets prepared by the Navigators. (These packets are also available through local Bible bookstores.)

Alternatively, you can use the simple "recipe card" technique shared by a young woman named Dana:

"My doctor told me I had to quit smoking during my first pregnancy, but several tries ended in defeat. I decided that part of the problem was the habit of my hands—I was in the habit of always reaching for a cigarette. Well, I copied 1 Cor. 10:13 onto several recipe cards and put them in the places where I used to keep my cigarettes—in my purse, beside my bed, etc. Every time I reached for a smoke, I found this truth:

" 'There is no temptation before you that is uncommon to others: but God is faithful, who will not let you be tempted above what you are able to bear.'

"And it worked! I was freed from an old and binding habit."

Other women have purchased cassette tapes that they can listen to while doing housework or driving to work. One woman wrote:

"During a time of extreme mental duress, someone suggested I fill my apartment with the sound of Scripture. My tapes of the New Testament became pretty worn out in the next few months, and something strong and wonderful began to happen in my mind. I was 'being cleansed by the washing of the water of the Word.'"

Determined Courage

Have you ever held so tightly to an object for so long—perhaps a garden rake or hoe—that your hand locked into position and it became almost impossible to put the object down?

In the book of 2 Samuel, we find some of the mightiest warriors who ever fought in the Israelite army. Eleazar was a soldier who defended his land with determined courage. He held onto his sword so tightly through a lengthy battle that, when the victory was complete, the sword could not be removed from his hand. In the words of Samuel, "His arm cleaved unto the sword." At the end of a day, a soldier like Eleazar would have to walk to a brook, laying his arm and sword in the water, letting the flow gently massage his hand until, one by one, the fingers could be pried from the sword.

What a graphic picture of how tightly we must hold onto

the sword of truth if we expect to gain personal victories in our own lives!

4. Nehemiah was patiently and consistently present; he laid "stone upon stone" until the work was complete.

"The problem with Western women," realized author Gail Sheehy after conducting extensive research for her book *Passages,* "is that they almost always tend to look for happiness and the answers to their problems outside of themselves! They look to lovers, to friends, to institutions, but not within."

But Nehemiah, a symbolic figure for the Holy Spirit, came to live *within* the city, partnering to see the work of rebuilding completed. Christianity gives the incredible picture of the Spirit of God at work within us. We are changed from the inside out. Jesus said, "How surely the Father will give the Spirit to them who ask Him."

One of the most important phases of Nehemiah's work was ensuring the permanent safety of a water source known as the King's Pool, or Hezekiah's well. The godly King Hezekiah had had his men dig an underground conduit through solid granite to bring life-giving water into the city from the Gihon Spring. Without this inner water, a hostile army could have simply surrounded the spring and forced the Israelites to come out of the fortified city. In the King's Pool (and the tunnel, which can be seen in Jerusalem today), we have an illustration of "the well of water that shall be in you, springing up into everlasting life" (John 4:14).

Following the resurrection, Jesus told his disciples, "Don't go anywhere or try to do anything until you have received the promised Holy Spirit."

Later in the New Testament, we are instructed to "be continually filled with the Spirit of God."

How wonderful, then, to realize that *self-control* is listed in Galatians as one of the Fruits of the Spirit. Self-control is a natural result of the Spirit-filled life!

When "Yes" Is "No!"

The subject of self-control, in any area of our lives, can be approached in two ways. We can begin with a list of don'ts, accenting the negative. Or, we can concentrate on the dos, accenting the positive path to self-control.

Phil. 4:8 is one list of positive biblical building blocks for self-control:

> *"Be full of the joy of the Lord . . .*
> *Fix your mind on whatever is true,*
> *whatever is good,*
> *whatever is right,*
> *Think about whatever is pure and lovely,*
> *and dwell on good news."*

Saying "yes" to the fullness of the Spirit is the best way to say "no" to habits that need changing.

Watchman Nee, the great Chinese Christian leader and martyr of this century, recorded a story in his journal about the power of the Holy Spirit to change the individual's life.

Nee was fleeing for his life from communist agents, traveling through remote mountain regions but stopping in tiny villages to preach the gospel message whenever he was able. In one village, he was welcomed into the home of the local leader.

The small hut was a shambles, filled with debris and confusion. The man was an alcoholic, a slave to the local brew; his mistreated wife watched Nee through sickly, half-crazed eyes. The children were filthy, anemic, and pitiful. But, after a day of conversation with Nee, both the man and his wife received the Lord into their hearts and asked for the presence of His Spirit.

Nee regretted that he could not stay longer. "Who will teach them how to live?" he worried. But he was a man with a price on his head—he was on his way before sunrise the next morning.

It was three years later when Nee was once again traveling that same footpath through the mountains. He stopped at the same home as before. He could hardly recognize the hut—it was so changed.

The father was sober and welcoming. The mother seemed whole and "in her right mind." The hut, though still humble, was swept and calm. The children were healthier, chattering and smiling at Nee with sparkling eyes.

"What missionary has come here?" Nee asked with joy. "Who has come and taught you how to live?"

The convert gave a simple but profound answer. Placing his hand on his heart and smiling, he said,

"INSIDE BOSS."

Songwriter Amy Grant has written a powerful song about the Holy Spirit's help in controlling fantasies:

> *"Faithless heart, be far away from me—*
> *Playing games inside my head that no one else can see.*
> *Faithless heart, you chill me to the core,*
> *But you don't have a hold on me*
> *So don't hang around any more.*

Chapter Eleven

The Beauty of
Balance

"We are no longer living just by the dictates of the flesh,
but in obedience to the promptings of the Spirit."
—Rom. 8:4; J. B. Phillips

MY son Benjamin was barely
two years old when he accomplished something that made him
feel like he had more muscles than Mr. T.

It was time for our Fourth of July supper, and our home
was filled with relatives. The tablecloth I wanted to use was
in the lowest drawer in the kitchen. Eight months pregnant,
I squatted awkwardly around my watermelon of a belly, digging in the drawer with one hand while clutching an assort-
ment of utensils in the other. Little Ben decided if I was down
on his level, I must be wanting to play. He walked up to my
right shoulder and gave a push.

In an instant, I found myself lying flat on the floor, utensils
clattering all around me, relatives gasping and rushing to help.
I was so embarrassed; I felt like a beached whale!

How could it happen? At any other time, I could have easily

withstood Ben's gentle push. But in the last weeks of pregnancy, like many women, I was totally lacking in *balance*.

Balance. It is the key factor in physical stability. It is also the key factor in emotional health.

For example, we need *balance* in our appetites. We can, on the one hand, crave food so much that we become obese. On the other hand, we can starve ourselves to the point of anorexia and serious illness. Or, with balance, we find food a source of both enjoyment and health.

Balance in our imagination. We can squelch this greatest of gifts or daydream so much that we are removed from reality— or we can channel daydreams into creativity.

Balance in our romantic fantasies. We can ignore this part of feminine sexuality or allow the flames to burn out of control— or we can find the healthy middle ground.

Balance between the human need for what is "new and exciting" and the other very real need for what is constant and changeless.

C. S. Lewis, in his classic *The Screwtape Letters,* gives insight into this last example of our need for balance. The book is a humorous satire, based on the efforts of Screwtape, a "senior devil," to teach Wormwood, a lowly devil, the art of temptation.

Screwtape tells Wormwood:

> The horror of "The Same Old Thing" is one of the most valuable lies we have introduced into the human heart. . . . The pleasure of novelty is by its very nature more subject than any other to the law of diminishing returns. . . .
>
> Since these humans experience time and must experience change, God has made change pleasurable to them. But since He does not wish them to make change, any more than eating, an end in itself, He has balanced the love of change in them with a love of permanence. He gives them the seasons, each season different yet every year the same, so that spring is always felt with novelty yet with the

recurrence of an immemorial theme. He has contrived, by the very world He has made, to show the union of change and permanence in the phenomenon of Rhythm.

The personality of each of us is made up of several equally important components. When all parts of life come together—the physical, mental, emotional, and spiritual—then we can live a life of balance, and come into the "abundant life" that the Creator meant for us to have. If the components of our being are not in balance, we can expect a roller coaster existence.

WONDERFULLY COMPLEX

A woman from Little Rock wrote with a question that could have been sent by thousands of women:

"Help! I feel like I am on a roller coaster. Sometimes I do all right, but sometimes I sink into the depths of depression. I am not sure if my problem is spiritual, or emotional, or physical. How in the world can I tell the difference? Why did God make me so complex? Who can tell me if my problem is in my spirit or my soul or my body?"

The answer she is seeking is the answer that a pastor seeks as he sits with a tearful counselee. The answer is one that a physician seeks as he considers the symptoms of a patient's illness, understanding that the mind affects the body and vice versa. The answer is the one sought by psychiatrists like M. Scott Peck, who writes, "Depending on the views of the counselor, there can be many varied diagnoses for the same person."

It is the answer being sought by many loving parents, like the woman who wrote: "Our daughter is on strong prescription drugs and has been for some time. When she comes home, she is so hateful to us that I almost believe that I am dealing with a demon. But maybe it's just that her body is a slave to those drugs, or maybe that her emotions are so frayed by her dependency. . . ."

The truth is that most of the time we are dealing with problems that have worked their way into *several* areas of our lives. Sometimes a problem begins in the emotional area but eventually becomes physical as well. Sometimes a problem that is initially physical throws us off balance in our mind and emotions.

Remember Psalm 139? "You made all the delicate, inner parts of my life, and knit me together in the womb. Thank you for making me so amazingly complex."

A human life cannot be easily divided into segments like the transparent overlays in the anatomy diagrams of medical textbooks. You are a unit, an incredible fusion of physical cells and eternal personality.

To come to true wholeness we must be willing to find balance between all of the areas of life.

It is interesting to know that the words *wholeness, health*, and *holy* come from the same Old English word.

Wholeness deals with well-being in the personality, the *emotional* realm.

Health deals with well-being in the body, the *physical* realm.

Holiness deals simply with well-being in the *spirit*—not an ethereal quality, but rather a soundness in one's relationship to the Creator.

THE LASER BEAM OF THE WORD

"The Word is quick [sharp] and powerful, dividing even between the soul and the spirit. . . ." Like a professional diagnostician, the Spirit can use the word of God to pinpoint our need, the area that is affecting all the other areas of our life. Like the sensitive laser used for surgery, the word of God can penetrate our deepest needs. Scripture can even give us discernment between what is emotional and what is spiritual.

• Lydia thought she had a spiritual problem. Several months

after a dramatic conversion to Christianity, Lydia went through a desert void of any "spiritual feeling." She worried that she was going to church and reading her Bible only as a habit. Then one morning she read the psalmist's description of a time when all his tears were dry, when his prayers seemed to be going nowhere. Lydia broke through in her understanding. She realized that, even though her emotions were at a "low," there was nothing wrong in her spiritual life. And with the psalmist she could say, "I know that God will restore to me the joy of my salvation."

• Another woman, June, became troubled by terrible bouts with her temper, and she sought emotional help from a wise Christian friend. The counselor listened to June's story, then turned to "for God understands our physical needs and takes compassion on us" (Heb. 4:15). She told June, "Your personality change has happened so quickly that I think it is physical, not emotional."

A thorough doctor's examination confirmed what the loving friend had suspected. June was suffering from severe hormonal imbalance, complicated by thyroid problems. June's husband was included in the discussions with the physician and began to understand the full extent of her needs.

• Jim found that he was reluctant to share his feelings with his new bride. "I could make love to her, but I could not talk to her. I thought my problem was that I was just emotionally cold. I was acting like the Gary Cooper man-of-few-words character.

"But one day after a very cool year in our marriage, I read 2 Tim. 1:7. I am not a good reader and it seems like I only get through a few verses at a time. But this one verse hit me right between the eyes. It almost knocked the wind out of me, because it was exactly what I needed: 'The Holy Spirit, God's gift, does not want you to be afraid of people, but to be wise and strong, and to love them and enjoy being with them.'

"My real trouble was that I had been listening to voices of fear. I was under a spiritual attack and didn't even know it. Lies of fear had told me that if I really shared myself with Lyla, she would laugh at me or think I was less manly. I have been rejecting those lies of fear, and I've discovered I am not really a 'cold husband' at all."

For each of these three individuals, Scripture became a personal diagnostician, and the tool they used for finding spiritual balance.

"For now we are cleansed throughout by the washing of the water of the Word" (Eph. 5:26).

BALANCE IN THE LIFE OF JESUS

In chapter two of Luke, we see that as Jesus matured, he "increased in wisdom [mentally] and stature [physically] and in favor with God [spiritually] and with man [emotionally and socially]." He was the living example of God's plan for a balanced, whole life.

IN WISDOM—MENTAL BALANCE

The following joke made the rounds at a convention of psychiatrists:

"One mental hospital has devised an unusual test to determine when patients are ready to go back into the world. The orderlies bring any candidates for release into a room where a tap is turned on and water is pouring out onto the floor. Next they hand the patient a mop and tell him to mop up the water. If the patient has forethought enough to turn off the tap *before* attempting to mop up the water, he is ready to go out into society. But if, as in the case of many, he tries mopping up the water while the tap is still running, then the directors know more treatment is needed!"

We laugh at that—and maybe we are laughing at ourselves! Hopefully we are learning to turn off the flood of wrong imaginings and wrong thinking that has been pouring into our lives, instead of continually mopping up the damage.

Yet mental balance in one's thought-life is so much more than that. Remember what Jesus said? Not "Be ye empty," but "Be ye filled"! With what? With the Spirit of God, and with the wisdom He brings. The book of Proverbs warns us often of the dangers of an idle mind. *In the fantasy survey, women listed mental boredom as one of the central factors contributing to excessive daydreaming.*

Having faith does not negate your intelligence. The Lord actually desires to increase your intelligence, and to augment and restore thought processes that are inactive. Since the "Jesus people" revival of the late sixties and early seventies, testimonies are common of God's restoration of minds that had been terribly damaged by drugs. The entire book of Joel gives the message that God wants to restore what has been lost.

Young King Solomon asked God for wisdom to rule his people, saying, "I don't feel intelligent enough, God, or mature enough for rulership. Please give me the mental capacity that only You can give." The Creator was so pleased with this request that Solomon became known as the most intelligent man in his day, and one of the wisest men of all time.

In the New Testament, we read: "If any of you lacks wisdom, ask God, for He delights in giving wisdom . . ." (James 1:5).

An Open Invitation

Do the romantic deluge and the erroneous thinking that come at us through the media mean you should break your television, stay away from all movies, and never read another love story as long as you live? Is the Bible the *only* literature one should read?

Absolutely not!

Great literature and art can nurture the God-given human capacity for beauty, for understanding, for compassion. It can put us in touch with things that are universal and elemental in human experience. It can *sharpen our focus, broaden our awareness, lift up our vision.*

T. S. Eliot, one of the towering figures of modern literature, believed that the Christian had to apply the moral and theological standards of the faith to all the "input" of his life. He taught that Christians should know how to read non-Christian literature without being swept into acquiescence as they read. Eliot wrote:

> It is simply this. If we, as readers, try to keep our religious and moral convictions in one compartment and take our reading (or viewing) merely for entertainment, or on a higher plane, for aesthetic value, I would point out that the author, whatever his conscious intentions in writing, in practice recognizes no such distinctions. The author of a work of imagination, such as a novel, is trying to move us wholly, whether he knows it or not, and we are affected by it, whether we intend to be or not.

Even "Christian literature" is not without its flaws. We have no examples of perfect Christian artists—but then, there was only one perfect Christian. We may never find one work of art that will perfectly satisfy both the theologians and the critics.

What is our position, then? Centuries ago, poet John Milton wrote that in our appreciation of the arts, we should learn to "piece together bits of perfection."

"Our job," says Eliot, "is to collect, to judge, to select those pieces that truly belong to God. We learn to assimilate the scattered truths that the artist communicates."

One literary giant who has used his mental capacities to their fullest is Aleksandr Solzhenitsyn. In a Siberian prison, where even the rudiments of his trade—paper and pencil—were taken from him, he learned to compose whole stories in his head, committing them to memory, editing them, and memorizing them again. Then he recited them to his fellow prisoners who, in turn, memorized them and repeated them to others for pure joy.

Solzhenitsyn says that probably he could "do all the important works all over again, from memory." And he adds that this active use of his mental faculties kept him sane in the insanity of prison confinement.

Regardless of some of Solzhenitsyn's religious views, we gain understanding from his insight into human nature. He doesn't need to call man "fallen" to show that he is. And Solzhenitsyn also shows such flashes of beauty, the "image of God" in his characters, that his writings put the theories of Marxist materialism to shame. No wonder he was banned by those who feared the faith!

The *Star Wars* saga has been one of the most influential fantasy-fairy tales of recent times. Many viewers were impressed with the Christian symbolism the films contained—the depiction of the battle between good and evil in the universe, the idea that the meek are victorious. But the *Star Wars* stories also contain mystical or superstitious overtones and some spiritual error. Can we be entertained by the films—by their special effects and happy endings—without taking in 100 percent the *theology* of the science fiction? Can we teach our children to do the same?

Each of us will have our own areas of sensitivity—in the last chapter we called these "allergies." Rom. 14:5 (J. B. Phillips) is a perfect verse regarding the need for each of us to find our balance in what we choose for mental input:

"One man thinks some things are more important, another

considers them all alike. Let each one be definite in his own convictions. Do so 'unto the Lord.'"

A car shifted into neutral will easily roll downhill; a mind shifted into neutral will do the same. We were not created for mental boredom; we were created to use our minds to the fullest, to "increase in wisdom." You must have mental challenge and quality mental stimulation. "It is the glory of God to conceal a truth in His universe, and the glory of man to discover it" (Prov. 25:2).

Willa wrote:

"I felt sorry for myself because of the mental tedium involved in being a stay-at-home mother with three little kids. I used it as an excuse to fill my days with soap operas and romantic daydreams.

"Then I met a new friend, Natalie. Once, when I dropped by, I noticed all the great books lying around her house—the kind of classics I haven't picked up since college. Another time, I found her sewing while her kids were taking their naps, and she was listening to 'Teach Yourself Swahili' tapes at the same time! 'Why Swahili?' I asked. 'Oh, I don't know,' she said. 'I just always was interested in trying it.'

"I left Natalie's house laughing, and with a new determination to find areas that are interesting to *this* young mother!"

IN STATURE—
PHYSICAL BALANCE

There is a great difference in the meaning of the words "amusement" and "recreation," even though we often use them interchangeably. The word "amusement" has little to do with thinking. For example, an amusement park is *not* a place you would go to to do serious thinking. The word "recreation," in contrast, has more to do with a restful activity that puts thing back into you—an activity that is *re-creative*. Most often, we think of recreation as physical activity.

In response to the survey, Lydia wrote a note about what she called a key to her mental well-being:

"I am one of those young women who has had a real tendency to live in a daydream world and a hard time accomplishing things in real life. I have found the greatest happiness in the past year since I have become involved in backpacking and mountain climbing. . . .

"I've been surprised to realize that this *hard, physical exercise* is actually helping me to control my *thinking*. I have realized that we modern men and women have so few activities that demand physical and mental concentration. Maybe this is part of the answer for other women—do things that make your body require this assistance of your mind."

Lydia is certainly not alone in her discovery. One California mental health clinic treats chronically depressed women with "walk therapy," requiring the women to take daily walks farther and faster than they would of their own initiative. The results reported have been phenomenal!

In its view of the physical body, Christianity differs from all of the other religions of the world. *God created our physical bodies; He loves them; He even plans to completely redeem them.* Some philosophies teach of an eternity in an endless "nirvana"—the Bible shocks us with the promise of the Resurrection.

Gnosticism, the Greek philosophy to which many of the statements in the New Testament are addressed, was wrapped in the belief that the physical body was evil and the soul or spirit of man good. At the opposite end of the spectrum, much of today's "religion" is that of body worship, which can also be called hedonism, or narcissism. Billions of dollars are spent annually on health spas, beauticians, and plastic surgeons.

In no area of our lives are we more in danger of being pushed out of balance. We can become anorexic or a picky health-food gourmet, or an overweight, unhealthy blob. We can worship the body and join the exercise cult, or our emotions can suffer because we ignore the body.

There are many simple points of balance in the physical realm that can affect all of the other areas of your life.

One area is simply that of understanding our own physical makeup. The psalmist said, "The Lord knoweth our frame and understands our frailties." But, too often, we don't know ourselves.

Do you know how much and what kind of exercise your body needs for your emotional happiness?

Do you know how much physical rest you need?

Sex therapists agree that one of the most common causes of sexual dysfunction in the female is *physical tiredness*. (As one woman in Chapter 3 wrote, It takes more energy to work on real sexual relationships than on fantasies.)

When the great prophet Elijah reached a time of personal despair, an angel appeared to minister to him. What was the earth-shaking message the angel brought to Elijah? "Sleep," the angel said, then "Eat some good food," then "Sleep" again. God understands us pretty well, doesn't He?

Do you understand your own monthly cycle and mood swings? Do you understand the physical season of life you are in now? Are you causing your body to work with you—or against you?

Dr. James Dobson lists some physical differences between men and women:

1. Men and women differ in every cell of their bodies. This difference in the chromosome combination is the basic cause of development into maleness or femaleness as the case may be.

2. Woman has greater constitutional vitality, perhaps because of this chromosome difference. Normally, she outlives man by three or four years in the U.S.

3. The sexes differ in their basal metabolism—that of woman being normally lower than that of man.

4. They differ in skeletal structure, woman having a

shorter head, broader face, chin less protruding, shorter legs, and longer trunk.

5. Woman has a larger stomach, kidneys, liver, and appendix, and smaller lungs.

6. In function, woman has several very important ones totally lacking in man—menstruation, pregnancy, lactation. All of these influence behavior and feelings. She has more different hormones than does man. The same gland behaves differently in the two sexes—thus woman's thyroid is larger and more active; it enlarges during pregnancy but also during menstruation; it makes her more prone to goiter, provides resistance to cold, is associated with the smooth skin, relatively hairless body, and thin layer of subcutaneous fat which are important elements in the concept of personal beauty. It also contributes to [emotions]—she laughs and cries more easily.

7. Woman's blood contains more water (20 percent fewer red cells). Since these supply oxygen to the body cells, she tires more easily, is more prone to faint.

8. In brute strength, men are 50 percent above women.

9. Woman's heart beats more rapidly (80, versus 72 for men); blood pressure (ten points lower than man) varies from minute to minute; but she has much less tendency to high blood pressure—at least until after the menopause.

10. Her vital capacity or breathing power is lower in the 7:10 ratio.

11. She stands high temperature better than does man; metabolism slows down less.

You are a unique and special creation. Your physical body, Paul wrote, has become the temple of the Holy Spirit. Are you taking care of this valuable temple?

"IN THE FAVOR OF GOD"—
BALANCE IN SPIRIT

In previous chapters we have talked about the area of the human personality that is most often ignored and unnourished—the spirit. Just as the physical body can be exercised and strengthened, we can be "strengthened with might in the inner man."

The miracle of the gospel is that it is both profoundly simple and unfathomably deep, so that a lifetime can be filled with fresh understanding and growing comprehension. In the last book of the well-known *Chronicles of Narnia,* this spiritual growth is called "going higher up and further in." The children in this symbolic fantasy enter a kingdom that seemed to have boundaries but, when entered, is revealed to contain "worlds within worlds." The higher up and further in the children go, the more the kingdom *expands*—its boundaries are infinite.

"God desires to work wholeness and balance in the spirit of an individual through many measures," writes Dr. William Backus, in his book *Telling Yourself the Truth.* "Among these are counseling, diet, rest, work, play, fresh air, fellowship, friends, human love and, at times, a psychotherapeutic relationship. He also works wholeness through the biblical methods of prayer, fasting, laying-on-of-hands, and deliverance."

The word "deliverance" has not yet been mentioned in this book, but it must be if we are to present a balanced view of the kind of transformation Jesus is willing to work in the spirit of those who come to Him. Some people are off balance because they blame too much on spiritual attack. They always complain that "the devil made me do it." Others are off balance because they leave no room in their theology for the discussion of deliverance. But deliverance was a part of the well-balanced theology of Jesus.

And in a book with words for those who may have entered the trap of pornography, or "given place to the evil one" (Eph. 4:27) in their imaginations, it must be included. "The forces which bind men and women in these days are strong forces," teaches psychologist Dr. M. Scott Peck. "We must give strong answers."

Connie wrote, "I have been involved in some pretty heavy things in my past . . . things that were occult and filled with darkness. I want to have a new mind and feel free, but to tell you the truth, I believe that I am dealing with evil spirits. I have heard the word 'deliverance,' but I am afraid to tell anybody that I think I need it. I don't know how to begin to pray, but I want to be free."

Like many people, Connie probably has the terrifying view of deliverance given by Hollywood in *The Exorcist,* and fear and confusion about terms like "demon possession" or "demon oppression." In reality, in the language of New Testament Greek, Jesus did not actually talk about "possession" or "oppression." In the original language, He reached out to those who were "troubled by evil forces" (Vine's *Greek and Word Studies*).

Jesus gives hope for freedom and wholeness. He said, "You shall know the truth, and the truth will set you free" (John 8:32). He said, "I give you power over all the power of the enemy, and nothing shall by any means hurt you" (Luke 10:19).

According to Ephesians, chapter 6, "The weapons of our warfare are not of the earth, but they are mighty in God for the pulling down of spiritual strongholds." The weapons are listed in verses 14–18, and the greatest is "the sword of the Spirit, which is the Word of God."

The only way to come against evil power is the method used by Christ Himself in Matthew, chapter 4, and Luke, chapter 4. Jesus spoke powerfully to His spiritual enemy by using the word of God. The wisest course of action for a woman who, like Connie, has been involved in a lifestyle filled with darkness, is to seek prayer with a pastor or mature Christian counselor who has a thorough knowledge of the word of God.

Yet each of us must at some time learn to use the weapon of the word for ourselves—or we will be totally defenseless, easily "pushed over" and thrown off balance. Each of us can discover the power in praying such verses as:

"Lord, in Your Name I renounce the hidden things of darkness" (1 Cor. 4:2).

"In Jesus' Name, I cast down imaginations, and every vain thing that exalts itself against the knowledge of God" (2 Cor. 10:5).

"Because of His work on the Cross, the Blood of Jesus the Son now cleanses us from all unrighteousness" (1 John 1:9).

"In Jesus' Name, I have authority over all the power of the enemy" (Luke 10:19).

As we grow in spiritual understanding of the Bible and we are "strengthened with might in the inner man" (Eph. 3:16), we will experience the balanced life that leads to wholeness. As our "spiritual muscles" are strengthened, they will begin to balance out the push of temptations and the strong physical demands of our nature. We will be women of balance.

There are so many faulty foundations upon which a woman can base her emotional life:

1. "The value of my life is based on the things that I do."
2. "The value of my life is based on what I possess."
3. "The value of my life is based on how I look."
4. "The value of my life is based on personal relationships."

These are only a few examples of false value systems which leave a woman looking outside of herself for emotional input. These faulty foundations produce an emotionally *dependent* woman, one who too often is an emotional drain on those closest to her because she has no inner balance.

On the other hand, there is great danger in saying "I do

not need others." Out of hurt, some of us have chosen a proud but dangerous and exaggerated *independence*. Our motto could be the "Gestalt Prayer" by Frederick S. Perls:

> *I do my thing and you do your thing,*
> *I am not in this world to live up to your expectations,*
> *And you are not in this world to live up to mine,*
> *You are you and I am I;*
> *If by chance we find each other*
> *It's beautiful.*
> *If not, it can't be helped.*

The balance of Christianity is neither the dependent woman who seeks fulfillment through other people nor the independent woman who seeks fulfillment only through herself and her romantic fantasies. The balance is found in what women's seminar leader Janet Congo has termed *interdependence. The interdependent woman has her emotional reservoir filled with the love of God; she is free to give love and to receive it.*

Marianne wrote:

"Within two years from the time my husband returned home from Viet Nam, I felt like my heart had been wrung out like a sponge. While we were struggling with his emotional scars, my own well got drained dry. I had no more tears and no more love, and absolutely no feelings of romance were left.

"But a wise friend told me to continue my loving *actions*. She said, 'Jesus told us simply "Love one another, not just in thought, but in word and deed." Have faith that God can refill your well of love.' And she was right. Feeling, true feeling, has followed my actions."

"Too often," wrote C. S. Lewis, "human beings have been encouraged to regard as the basis for marriage a highly colored and distorted version of something [romance] that God actually promises as its result."

The underlying principle of human emotions is that they

fluctuate. A child can go from extreme highs to extreme lows in a matter of seconds—and many adults don't take much longer! Changes in the weather, changes in our health, the daily news, an incident in the house—the many events in just one day can make us feel like a human trampoline.

The journey to emotional balance is one of *choice*. It is aided greatly if the other areas of life—the mental, the physical, and the spiritual—are *in balance*. The woman of stability has made firm decisions:

> *She is choosing to have faith instead of fear.*
> *She is choosing to love but not to lean.*
> *She is choosing to soar like an eagle but not to become proud.*
> *She is choosing to accept her femininity without denying or degrading masculinity.*
> *She is choosing to be positive instead of negative.*
> *She is choosing to be a woman with dreams and vision, yet a woman who is fully alive today, alive in reality and not just in fantasy.*

For three generations, the famous Wallenda family has thrilled audiences around the world with stunning feats of balance. An expert on the high wire, Karl Wallenda has helped train twenty other family members. In a television interview, he was asked, "Do your family members inherit this incredible balance?"

"No child is born with perfect balance," he replied. "Balance is the result of training and practice. *Balance must be learned.*"

Chapter Twelve

Step into the Sunshine

We need have no fear of someone who loves us
perfectly; His perfect love for us eliminates all dread of
what He might do to us. If we are afraid, it is for fear of
what He might do to us [fear of His will], and shows
that we are not yet fully convinced that God really
loves us.

—1 John 4:18; The Living Bible

EVERY human being yearns
to love and be loved, and to be loved perfectly. Connected to
this longing for love, and woven into every cell of our being,
is our human sexuality. For both men and women, *sexuality
is not only physical; it is emotional and deeply spiritual*.

In the years just before the outbreak of World War II, one
wise and wealthy man foresaw the terror that was to come.
He poured his life savings into the purchase of part of a tiny,
secluded South Pacific island. He thought he had found the
perfect escape. The island's name? Guam! Within a year,
World War II was on his doorstep!

Most of us are like that unfortunate man. We prefer to avoid any involvement in conflict—not just physical conflict, but also mental and emotional conflict or spiritual conflict. So when it comes to our fantasies, our secret sexual thoughts, our emotions, we wish we could simply live with them in a state of peaceful nirvana. We don't want to confront them.

I grew up exposed to romance from all the media—I read gothic novels and romantic classics, watched soaps on TV, was a pushover for movies that were tearjerkers, and knew the lyrics to many romantic songs.

But eventually, one fact became absolutely clear to me: I was involved in an ongoing battle for the control of my thoughts and emotions.

This clarity didn't come right away. When I first became a Christian, I was a conscientious objector. I wanted no part of this spiritual war. After all, I was from the generation of determined pacifists, draft-card burners, and flower children. I objected to the spiritual war which engulfed my emotions. I had wanted to live in a sea of tranquillity. As a believer, I felt that I could choose the lilies of the field and brotherly love and all of the other soothing aspects of the gospel message. Then, like the unfortunate man who lived on Guam during World War II, I found myself standing in the front lines of a battlefield, flaming missiles exploding all around me.

I had no helmet. I carried no shield. In the book of Ephesians, I read that I was to take up the sword. "Sword?" I gasped. "Was I issued a sword?"

I decided that I had better find out. In the war for our emotions, I soon discovered, even those of us who wanted to be conscientious objectors have been drafted! *The war is on our doorsteps—in fact, it has moved beyond our doorsteps, and is being waged in our hearts and minds.*

When I became a professional counselor, I began to meet many women whose lives have been affected by the romantic deluge. I met women such as Summer O'Brian, whose story is told in Chapter 2. I met women such as Rene, who says in her letter included in the preface to this book, that she has a good husband and yet has not been "content or satisfied."

Finally, I began to question women across the United States, using the fantasy survey. I immersed myself in this subject because I wanted to know more about the imagination and modern feminine sexuality.

I end the book with only a *partial* understanding of the deluge of romantic fantasy on women—to claim more than that would be unforgivably dishonest. To say one has a "great" understanding of fantasy and human sexuality would be to limit the limitless power of human creativity, to deny the immeasurableness of that awesome quality in which we are most like God!

In this chapter, we will simply review some of the conclusions that can be drawn from the response to the survey, and we will look at a few final implications of the power of the human imagination.

SOME CONCLUSIONS

#1. For many modern women, it is extremely difficult to "live in reality."

For some, there is the nagging temptation to "check out" mentally during the normal routine, to anesthetize feelings when the going gets rough, or to live vicariously through television and romantic novels.

One cause for "opting for fantasy," especially in younger women, may be the anxiety of living in the nuclear age, with its portents of doom and destruction. Another cause is a life that has become too tedious or too complicated, with few reprieves from the routine.

However, the most important cause contributing to an over-dependence on fantasy, especially sexual fantasy, is that we live in a society where we receive an incredible amount of fantasy input. Earlier, we read from the letter of a woman who had said that every time she turned on the television or opened a magazine, there were these stories of great sex outside of marriage. She began to think she was the *only one* who had not been involved in a torrid affair.

The woman continued: "As I participate in this survey, I realized that I am not alone in the way I have been affected in my fantasies by the bombardment of sexual eroticism. It is like the verse in 1 Peter 4:12: 'There has come upon you no strange affliction that differs from what other believers face at this time.' In this time, fantasies that are out of control are 'no strange affliction.'"

In modern society, self-discipline and self-control are no longer emphasized; we have settled into a lifestyle of *"choosing the easy way out."* We are accustomed to fast-food restaurants and drive-through banks and eyeglasses-in-one-hour. As one woman quoted earlier wrote, "I have to admit that my reason for fantasizing so much is that it is *easier to deal with a person in your imagination than to work out a relationship with a flesh-and-blood man.*"

The result of all this as Mike Mason states in his book *The Mystery of Marriage*: "People are continually being hoodwinked into assuming they are in a relationship with one another, when really all they are relating to is themselves!"

Whatever the reason to escape reality, fantasy living becomes progressively easier in the modern world of mass media. (The latest statistics show that the majority of American homes subscribe to cable television networks, and in 1990, a full 80 percent of viewers receiving cable had opted to receive the erotic channels that are offered!) Many pop songs, movies, and magazine articles will subtly push us toward mental *voyeurism*—toward observing sex in the medium of our own fantasies.

#2. Today's woman has exaggerated views of what life should hold, of what love and romance should be.

A woman from Green River, Wyoming, wrote:

"One day, I complained to my husband, 'Why don't you treat me the way other men treat the women they love?'

" '*What* other men?' he asked simply.

"I couldn't reply, because I suddenly realized that the 'other men' I wanted him to act like were not any men that we knew, but the male characters in a series of romance novels I had been reading. I was comparing my real man to an author's made-up image of a man!"

As another woman wrote in a letter quoted earlier, "No flesh-and-blood man can act like or measure up to a fairy-tale prince."

Recall that in Nancy Friday's *My Secret Garden,* she reports sexual fantasies from dozens of women, but near the end of the book, she gives one woman's honest advice: "Don't make the mistake of thinking you can live out a fantasy. *Believe me, your fantasies, acted out in reality, can be life's greatest disappointment . . .*"

Dagmar O'Connor, director of sexual therapy at St. Luke's-Roosevelt Hospital in New York, has seen how exaggerated views of love and romance lead to problems. "I deal with many individuals who wrongly believed that some new relationship would meet all their emotional needs," she says. "No 'affair of the heart' can make your life wonderful; only *you* can—by being open with your feelings and sexual needs, by acknowledging your emotional needs to your mate, and working through the nitty-gritty problems of any real-life relationship."

#3. Different women have different points of emotional vulnerability.

Consider these different opinions expressed by four women:

• "I can watch a great romance without wanting to trade places with the heroine. I love to experience these mental trips that give me understanding of other places, other times, other societies. For me, romantic input is *not* a problem."

• "As a widow, I must say that the kind of *good* romantic

novels I choose to read are not wrong. The aspects of culture traditionally reserved for women—loving, nurturing, selflessness—all of these are often a part of old-fashioned romances. If a woman *chooses* carefully, the romance novel allows its readers to celebrate these values without apologies."

• "I am one of those people really affected by what I see— I am like a *sponge*. If I watch soaps or sexy movies, I become dissatisfied with my own good-but-routine life, dissatisfied with my good, dependable husband."

• "How can we say that what we see doesn't affect us? Jesus taught 'The eye is the lamp of the body. If your eye is good, your whole body will be full of light' (Matt. 6:22)."

As these quotes show, women are vulnerable to different extents. Sometimes, though, it's hard to know the extent of your own vulnerability.

One of the first women I ever counseled about "romantic input" was a personal friend and neighbor I will call Colleen. Pretty and vivacious, in college she often had more offers for dates than she could accept. Then she married a charming, good looking classmate and settled down to live happily ever after.

A year later, she called one afternoon and invited me over for coffee. "Could you pray for me?" she asked as we were talking. "John is a good husband, but I feel bored and depressed and not nearly as happy as I expected to be."

We talked about the importance of our thought-life and about how real love cannot cause the continual, high-pitched surge of emotions described in romantic fantasies. I had already noticed that her bookshelf was lined with gothic romances. Perhaps, I suggested, she should stop reading so many romantic novels. Colleen agreed to but thought it would make no difference.

Two months later, my friend called with a report of her growing happiness. "I got rid of all of those books," Colleen told me, "and I can't believe the difference! I guess I just wasn't living in reality. I wasn't seeing how blessed I really am; I wasn't concentrating on developing romance with this man God has given me. Even John has noticed the difference in my contentment and happiness. He said, *'I feel like you love me more lately.'* "

Reading a novel filled with romance or a great fictional story is not wrong. But for Colleen, these books *became* wrong; in fact, in her life, they became a form of bondage. She lived in the imagined world so often that her *real world was suffering*.

Some women are more vulnerable in other areas of their imagination. Here are two examples from survey responses:

"For me, the input that I must avoid is anything that feeds my natural tendency to be fearful. I guess a lot of women can watch scary shows or read Stephen King, but if *I* do, my imagination runs away with me, and my vivid imagination causes me to suffer."

"I am a musician, and I guess this is why I am so moved by whatever music I listen to. . . . A song can leave me feeling depressed or rebellious or happy, so I have to be careful about the music that I listen to. It sets the tone for my whole day."

"I can do anything I want to if Christ has not said no, but some of these things just aren't good for me" (1 Cor. 6:12, *The Living Bible*).

#4. The imagination is the richest of gifts, the creative treasure meant to be used to enhance your present and your future.

In earlier pages, we quoted women who have come to understand the creative uses of their imaginations. *Creative problem solving* and imaginative thinking can help us fill our futures with hope. Women who had felt trapped in an unfulfilling job have creatively moved into *careers that meet their inner dreams and desires*. Women who had felt overwhelmed by the task of raising children have made their lives easier by *creative scheduling*. Women who had allowed their marriage to fall into the boredom of routine have used their creativity to *plan romantic interludes*.

The imagination *heightens our enjoyment* of the arts and good literature. Since the imagination is tied to our memory, it also enables us to recall the past, allowing us to *relive important moments* and *enrich the present*. Our imagination can also help us to *avoid mistakes* in the future; for this reason, speakers will often ahead of time imagine themselves performing their speech.

For a young person, the imagination allows a *rehearsal* of another kind—the rehearsal of romance. The person works out answers to the question "How will I react to love when I find it?"

As a part of sexuality, the imagination is designed to *enhance lovemaking* with your spouse and *enrich marital fulfillment*. Although if uncontrolled, the imagination can weaken the sense of marital oneness, when centered on your mate it can create a sense of *"delicious longing."*

Author Charlie Shedd says, "Anticipation is one of God's good gifts. When I think of my wife, I say, 'I can hardly wait. Tonight we celebrate our love!' For the wise couple, thinking about sex ahead of time, gradually *turning up the thermostats* is a part of great sex."

#5. Because we are affected by our fantasies and daydreams, it is important, from time to time, to reexamine our thought-life.

These quotes, from three survey responses, address the importance of examining our thought-life:

"I didn't realize where my imagination had led me. . . . I had fantasized so much that I became bored with my real life. An old boyfriend came to see me, and I almost ran away with him, leaving my husband and children. Then I came to my senses and saw this old flame for who he is and always has been—an undependable man who could never really love me as my husband loves me. The trouble really started long before the old boyfriend arrived—it started in my imagination. There is a Latin proverb that really applies to the imagination, and I think your readers will profit from it. . . .

" 'Corruptio optima pessima' or
" '*The best thing, used wrongly, becomes the worst thing.*' "

"I took the survey, and then I stopped to realize how affected I have been by all of the illusions of romance that I have watched and read about. Slowly, subtly, I have been drawn into a very wrong way of thinking, thinking that is selfish and filled with 'me-ism.' I have assumed, wrongly, that a good lover will automatically meet all of my romantic longings."

"Examining our fantasies, and then letting go of things that are wrong is really difficult; but that is what the Bible encourages us to do, isn't it? David wrote, 'Search me, O God, and know my heart; try me and know my thoughts, and see if there be any wicked way in me, and lead me in the way everlasting' (Ps. 139:24)."

Columnist Abigail Van Buren writes, "Many people know part of the Alcoholics Anonymous prayer that says 'Just for today, help me to change those things which can be changed and accept those things I cannot change.' My version of this is, 'Just for today, I will face reality.' For many women, my best counsel is . . . 'From time to time, we must re-decide to *face reality.*' "

#6. *Human sexuality and imagination are part of God's good plan; the guidelines He gives flow out of His love.*

Many readers may be wondering what eventually happened to Summer, the woman whose story is given in detail in Chapter 2. It is wonderful to be able to end this conclusions section with a letter from Summer:

"For over ten years now, I have been happily married to Bill Harvey. Bill certainly did not look or act like the man in my fantasies, but he truly is my Prince Charming in every sensē of the word. I once asked if it was worth it to give up the perfection of imaginary lovers for the imperfections of a flesh-and-blood man. All I can say is that love in reality is better than a mirage. Sustaining romance in reality is not easy, but it is so worthwhile. Now I have 'the real diamond' whereas once all I had was a cheap counterfeit.''

"Bringing a mind that was out of control back into control is really difficult. All of us have some battles with our imaginations. Giving up old habits really hurts, but it is worth it. There is a wonderful illustration from *Pensées,* that classic work by Pascal:

> Our hearts sometimes feel torn asunder by opposing efforts. But it would be very unfair to impute this struggle to God, who is drawing us on, instead of to the world, which is drawing us back. We are like a child whose mother tears it from the arms of harm-intending kidnappers, in the pain it suffers,—that child would love the legitimate force of one who procures its liberty, and detest only the tyrannical violence of those who would detain it unjustly.

"I find myself being pulled forward by 'the One who loves me perfectly,' and I have no fear of living God's way any longer. 'His perfect love eliminates the fear of what His will is.' (1 John 4:18; The Living Bible).

"I know now that when He tells us in Ecclesiastes to 'be continually enraptured by your mate,' and 'drink water from your own cistern,' He calls us to emotional faithfulness because He loves us. I know now that when He tells us to 'cast down harmful imaginations,' He does so because He loves us.''

Mike Mason, in *The Mystery of Marriage,* writes powerfully about the sexual relationship:

> What can equal the surprise of finding out that the one thing above all others which mankind has been most proficient in dragging through the dirt turns out to be the most innocent, clean thing in the world? Is there any other activity which an adult man and woman may engage in together (apart from worship) that is more childlike, more free and pure, more natural and wholesome and unequi-

vocably right than is the act of lovemaking? For if worship is the deepest form of communion with God, then surely sex is the deepest communion that is possible between human beings, and as such is something absolutely essential to our survival. . . .

When we feel we are caught in the steel trap of marriage, we may do a lot of squirming and struggling. *Over and over, we must wake up to the fact that there is only one way to get untrapped, and that is to relax and start learning more about love, more about sexuality, than we ever wanted to know.*

To clearly show the *goodness* of the biblical view of a woman and her sexuality, some therapists such as Mary Ann and Joseph Mayo have charted Christianity against other prevailing world views:

Model	View of a Woman	Relationship to Man	Fulfillment or Salvation	Marriage
Patriarchal societies	Valued for breeding, a servant	Property of man	By childbearing	Necessity
Hedonism	*Playboy* "bunny"	Sexual partner	By orgasm and eroticism	Sometimes convenient
Feminism	Self-sufficient career woman	Rival, or competitor	By asserting independence	Contract to serve ambitions
Romanticism	Fairy princess	Object of men's dreams	Possessed by "knight"	Possibly a threat (if it interferes with "true love")
Scriptural	Unique creation "in God's image"	Beloved helpmate, "joint heir of the kingdom"	Understanding God's love, discovering His purpose	A fulfilling partnership, building God's kingdom, entrusted with children

A SHADOW OF THINGS TO COME

We were created for creativity.

"O fantasy, that at times doth snatch us out of Ourselves, so that we are conscious of naught. . . . Who makes thee, if the world sets naught before thee? A Light moves thee which takes its form in heaven, of Himself, or by His will that sendeth it down" (Dante, *The Divine Comedy*).

"The problem in America is not the use of the imagination. The problem is the narrowness of its use. Too often the imagination is employed almost solely for themes that are erotic." When Solzhenitsyn spoke these words on an American college campus, he went on to say that the majority of Americans and Europeans are not as "free" in their imagination as they think they are, because their fantasies as a whole are very restricted, usually based on me-ism. "How wonderful if this generation was truly free in the area of imagination—free to discover all of the good, God-given uses of fantasy."

God asks us to carefully treasure our creativity, for our happiness and the happiness of those around us. But He has plans that reach far beyond today's happiness. We are created to be eternal creatures. Perhaps God wants us to learn control of our imaginations now, to become trustworthy in our creativity now, because of an *eternal plan for this awesome ability*.

The Bible says that "eye has not seen, nor ear heard, neither have entered into the heart of man the things which God has prepared for them that love Him" (1 Cor. 2:9). He has created "worlds without end"; He plans for His children to rule and reign with Him (Rom. 5:17b).

What if a part of that rulership includes *creative rulership*? What if the joy that comes to an interior designer as she furnishes a lovely home is only a shadow of the joy of furnishing a new world? What if the joy experienced by an expert gardener at spring's first roses is only a shadow of the joy of landscaping a new continent? In the age to come, our imaginations and fantasies may be backed with true creative power.

What worlds can you envision?

What creative abilities would thrill your soul?

Steven Spielberg, when asked about the creative marvels he had built in his *Star Wars* studio, said, "Yes, it's coming together, but the building is so tedious. If only my ideas had wings!"

Steven, there may come a day . . .

"Christian artists do not need to be threatened by fantasy and imagination," wrote Francis Schaeffer. "The Christian is the one whose imagination would fly beyond the stars."

The Deepest of Heart's Desires

If earthbound imaginations are only a shadow of things to come, how much more do the deepest of our heart's desires point us toward an eternal fulfillment?

Philosophers the world over have discovered what Nietzsche termed "a God-shaped vacuum in the heart."

If we do not know God, we create a god. The "God-shaped vacuum" causes some to delve into the occult, searching for a source for power beyond us. Others have the god of science. (Shortly before George Bernard Shaw died, he wrote that the counsels of science were his faith and that faith had failed him completely.)

The Bible tells us that for some, their "god is their own belly"—that is, some "worship their own cravings and passions." They try to fill their God-shaped vacuum by worshiping sensuality and sexual fantasy, thinking the vacuum can be filled with love or desire for another person.

Admittedly, some attempts at filling the vacuum work better than others, yet with any, pieces of our inside puzzle are missing. "But everything that exists in Heaven or earth shall find its perfection and fullness in Him" (Eph. 1:10; J. B. Phillips).

Eternity in My Heart

Besides the restless longing for fullness in our God-shaped vacuum, the feelings that we have point to a subconscious longing for eternity. Somehow, men and women everywhere sense "I was meant for *more* than this."

In an earlier chapter, we saw comments from women who had fallen into sentimental lies, into a longing for "the good old days." We get angry that good times pass quickly. We are irrationally angry at our bodies when they begin to break down. We moan about every wrinkle, about the loss of youthful beauty. We are disappointed when passions lose some of their original fire. Why are we so unreasonable? Partly because throughout all history, *mankind has had a subconscious knowledge that in original creation, we were created to be changeless.*

In nothing are we more resistant to change than in the separations that are forced by physical death. Death is a hated enemy.

We ache when we hear of the death of a child, and say, "It's not fair! The child had only begun to live." We cringe when we hear of the death of a teenager, and say, "It's not fair! He was in the prime of life." We groan when we learn of the passing of a young mother, "It's not fair! Her children needed her so desperately." Even when a dear grandparent slips from this world after many full years, we grieve. "It's not fair!" we cry. "I wanted her around forever. I can't imagine life without her."

It's not fair. Something deep in the core of our being rises up in violent protest of death and of the separation it brings. It is as if our subconscious mind whispers, "Man was not created for this."

Our natural response to death and final separation flow out of an unexplainable, inborn desire to be eternal. Perhaps we do not recognize it with our conscious mind, but in our subconscious, we cry out for the *perfection of eternity*; we were created for this, and for nothing less!

Christians have sometimes tried to soften the impact of death, speaking of "crossing the Jordan," or trying to portray death as a friend that comes to convey us from a troubled world into heaven. Maybe somehow it has been implied that this is a spiritual view of death. But you do not have to see death as anything less than what it is—the enemy that takes those we love and leaves us with pain.

Jesus did not paint a rosy picture of death, nor call it a friend. He saw death as an enemy to battle on our behalf. In fact, He wept with anguish at the grief physical death brings to a family (John, chapter 11).

Scripture tells us that the Son of God came to destroy all the works of darkness, and that "the last Enemy which shall be destroyed is death." Jesus came in the flesh to regain for those of us who live in the flesh "the keys of death" (Rev. 1:18).

Death is in reality a painful separation. Because the original sin brought sickness and decay into the world, death has come to claim mankind and bring eternal separation between you and God, between you and your loved ones. But through His finished work on the cross, Christ can now override the claims of sin on mankind and therefore override death.

When death reaches out a chilling hand to steal away a life, Christ's strong grasp of love overrules the hand of destruction. "Oh, death!" Christ proclaims. "This one is mine!"

This is why 1 Cor. 15:55 says, "O death, where is now thy sting?"

Human nature resists death and separation more than anything else, but to some extent, we also resist other changes. In

Chapter 4, we mentioned the need for adventure and excitement, but even the most adventurous of us long to keep some things "intact." We get extremely sentimental about the days of our childhood. We don't want the "old homestead" to look any differently. We wish our grade school hadn't been torn down. We may long for an earlier time when life was simpler. We are gripped by nostalgia when we hear an old sweet song. We try to keep our bodies from changing, to push back the processes of aging which changes the steel strength of youth to the dryness of brittle bones. We wish a romantic relationship could maintain a constant, high-pitched, feverish passion. We are ever unsuccessful in our attempts to "keep things from diminishing."

This inner longing for a world in which time does not slip through our fingers points us to our eternal purpose.

LONGING FOR THE PERFECT LOVE

Many have ridiculed women who have what has been called "the Cinderella syndrome." But men have it, too: "I have this elusive dream of finding a love that will completely fulfill me," wrote a Harvard senior when he responded to the survey. "I wanted to get in on this survey because I'll have you know that *men have their share of romantic longings, too!* For the most part, we are afraid to express them. But I dream of the *Perfect Love,* someone who will stand by me through thick and thin. Someone who is beautiful inside as well as out. Someone who is interesting and great fun to be around. Most of all, someone who would never betray me."

"Someday my prince will come," sang Snow White in the classic Disney version of the familiar fairy tale. "Someday all dreams come true."

In this story, Snow White has fallen prey to the jealous hatred of a demonic queen. She is tricked into eating the poisoned fruit and falls for years into the coma of the sleeping death. The kingdom groans with the grief of its loss until the prince arrives. He kneels beside Snow White humbly and kisses her with life-restoring love.

The prince lifts her to his white horse, and they ride together into a glorious sunset, the horse rising above the clouds to a castle that glistens. The prince has taken his beloved to the Happy-Ever-After that could not be found in an earthly domain.

Women who treasured this story as little girls and have felt broken as it eluded them in adult relationships have yet to discover the *symbolic theme* woven into this most famous of fairy tales.

Annie Herring, award-winning singer and songwriter, grew up clinging to the hope of "love ever after" and a Prince Charming. "How I had loved fairy tales as a child," Annie recalls, "but in a series of crises, my dreams were smashed out of me." Then Annie's life was changed completely. In a simple prayer of salvation, she discovered there was One who could love her perfectly.

Annie, with her sister Nellie and brother Matthew, went on to found the Second Chapter of Acts, a Christian pop group that has written and recorded many songs and sold millions of records. "But my entire testimony is best described in the words of one of my first songs," Annie says. The song is this:

> *You know a story, though you've heard it a time or two,*
> *About a Prince who kissed a girl right out of the blue.*
> *Hey, this story ain't no tale to me now—*
> *For the Prince of Peace has given me life somehow.*
> *You know what I mean.*

There is a Prince yet to come. There is One who has the power and the authority to save us from the sleeping death. There is One who has not forgotten us, who has a plan for

Happiness-Ever-After, a plan that includes ruling and reigning at His side in a limitless domain.

At His first appearance, "He humbled himself, and came dressed as a servant" (Phil. 2:7–8).

But, at His return, His kingdom will come in power and glory. In the book of Revelation, we see a picture of the Prince of Peace returning on the white horse, the event which is often symbolized in fairy tales.

And when that day comes, we will finally be the perfect beauty that is also at the core of so many of our romantic daydreams. "I imagine myself as different," was a common response to the survey. One day, we will be the Bride "without blemish or flaw" (Eph. 5:27). We will be changed (1 Cor. 15:52). "My friends, we are not yet sure what we shall be like but we know we shall be like Him, for we will see Him as He really is" (1 John 3:2).

Your longing for the perfect love is an intuitive, subconscious longing for what we will one day know. It is something God has placed within each of us, an explicable yearning that is meant to draw us, not in frustrating circles, but to Him.

A silent inner calling. Wordless, yet compelling. Inexpressible, but real.

C. S. Lewis used a book of fantasy called *The Screwtape Letters* to imagine how it will be when we finally stand in the presence of One who loves us perfectly. C. S. Lewis was an Oxford don, a professor of literature at Cambridge, and the most widely read Christian philosopher of the twentieth century. His best-selling books include the ever-popular *Chronicles of Narnia, Mere Christianity,* and *The Space Trilogy.*

Earlier we quoted briefly from *The Screwtape Letters.* In the final chapter of this delightful narrative, Lewis describes the final fulfillment of all of our inexplicable inner longings. Screwtape, the senior devil, writes a scathing letter to Wormwood, the junior devil he instructs, because Wormwood's assigned human has died, and thus slipped through their hellish influence forever:

> You have let a soul slip through your fingers. The howl of sharpened famine for the loss of that soul re-echoes at this moment through all the levels of the Kingdom of Noise down to the very Throne of Hell itself. It makes me furious to think of it. . . .
>
> How well I know what happened at the instant when [the angelic spirit-beings] snatched him from you! There was a sudden *clearing* of his eyes (was there not?) as he saw you for the first time, and recognized the part you had had in him and knew that you had it no longer. Just think (and let it be the beginning of your agony) what he felt at that moment; as if a scab had fallen from an old sore, as if he were emerging from a hideous, shell-like tetter, as if he shuffled off once and for all a defiled, wet, clinging garment. By Hell, it is misery enough to see them in their mortal days, taking off dirtied and uncomfortable clothes and splashing in hot water and giving little grunts of pleasure— stretching their eased limbs! What then of this final strip-ping, this complete cleansing?
>
> The more one thinks about it, the worse it becomes. He got through it so easily! No gradual misgivings, no doctor's sentence, no nursing home; rather sheer instantaneous lib-eration [the man had been killed in the London bombings]. One moment it seemed to be all our world; the scream of bombs, the fall of houses, the stink and taste of high ex-plosives on the lips and in the lungs, the feet burning with weariness, the heart cold with horrors, the brain reeling; next moment all this was gone, gone like a bad dream, never again to be of any account.
>
> Defeated, out-maneuvered fool! Did you mark how nat-urally—as if he's been *born* for it—the earth-born vermin entered the new life? How all his doubts became, in the twinkling of an eye, ridiculous? I know what the creature

was sighing to itself! "Yes, of course, it was always like this. All horrors have followed the same course, getting worse and worse and forcing you into a bottleneck till, at the very moment when you thought you must be crushed, you were out of the narrows and all was suddenly well. . . . You die and die and then you are beyond death. How could I ever have doubted it?"

As he saw you, he also saw [the angelic spirit-beings]. I know how it was. You reeled back dizzy and blinded, more hurt by them than he had ever been by bombs. The degradations of it!—that this things of earth and slime could stand upright and converse with spirits before whom you, a spirit, could only cower. Perhaps you had hoped that the awe and strangeness of it would dash his joy. But that is the cursed thing, the *Spirit-beings are strange to mortal eyes, yet they are not strange.* He had no faintest conception till that very hour of how they would look, and even doubted their existence. But when he saw them he knew that he had always known them and realized what part each one of them had played at many an hour in his life when he had supposed himself alone. So now he could say to them one by one, not "Who are you?" but *"So, it was YOU all the time!"*

All that they were and said at this meeting woke memories. The dim consciousness of friends about him which had haunted his solitudes from infancy was now at last explained; *that central music in every pure experience* which had always just evaded memory was now at last recovered. Recognition made him free in their company almost before the limbs of his corpse became quiet. Only you were left outside.

He saw not only Them;
he saw Him.

This low one, this thing begotten in a bed, could look on Him. What is blinding, suffocating fire to you is now cool light to him, is clarity itself, and *wears the form of a Man.*

You would like, if you could, to interpret the patient's prostration in the Presence, his self-abhorrence and utter knowledge of his sins (yes, Wormwood, a clearer knowledge even than yours) on the analogy of your own choking and paralyzing sensations when you encounter the air that breathes from the heart of heaven. . . . But all the delights of sense or heart or intellect with which you could once have tempted him . . . now seem to him in comparison as the half-nauseous attractions of a raddled harlot would seem to a man who hears that his true beloved, whom he has loved all his life and whom he had believed to be dead, *is alive and even now at his door*.

This is a picture from a truly inspired imagination, a picture to be read again and again.

The quality and completion of the Love that is set before us gives joyful meaning to life. We live in anticipation of our inheritance. Love has a greater destiny than human hearts can ever imagine.

Many of us have resented the theological notion that the relationships of earth will be done away with in heaven, since Jesus said that there is no marriage, as we know it, in heaven. "In heaven we will have a different kind of glory" (1 Cor. 13). He did not say that love will be done away with—rather, that it will *change*. The deepest love of this age may be only a *foreshadowing* of the age that is to come! Love will not be negated—it will be multiplied to the nth degree!

Just as an unborn child is fully alive in the womb and then is born into a world far bigger than could have been imagined in the womb, we now are in the womb of existence in this life, and we will one day be born into a world far greater than we have dared dream. The feelings you have for your loved ones will not diminish: they will rather reach a height and fullness never known in this lifetime. Now we experience passions that are pulled down by gravity, laced with the earthly law of diminishing returns—there the thrill of passions will never diminish!

Does this great expectation take away from the quality of love that can grow between a man and a woman right now? Just the opposite. It expands it! The entire book of 1 John says over and over again:

"Because He first loved us, we are *really free now* to love each other."

After looking at the response of hundreds of women to the fantasy survey, after searching for wisdom from the biblical perspective, we close this book with insight not from a master storyteller, like C. S. Lewis, not from a gifted theologian, but from the everyday housewife whose letter in the preface opened this book:

"Until I thought about the impact of romantic fantasy on modern women, I had never connected my discontentment in marriage with the things I imagined. I never realized that I have been living with subtle delusions. I didn't know I was asking my husband to measure up to a mirage.

"Romantic screen images like *Casablanca* are images that have been shared by millions. But the reality of *this day* is unique to me. Not even my husband shares it—he sees it from a different perspective. Last night as I lay in bed, watching my husband sleeping gently beside me, feeling movement of a new baby that is growing in me, I was overwhelmed by the thought, 'This is a moment only *I* can experience.'

"*I do not want the precious moments of reality to slip through my fingers.*

"*I am learning to be more sensuous in reality, not just in my imagination.* . . . Our fantasies are a powerful tool, and I want to use them in the right ways.

"I just want to say thank you (and my husband thanks you, too!). My new understanding of spiritual warfare as it applies to everyday thinking is a real key to happiness. And in the long run, I believe it will save both my marriage and my sanity.

"I feel like, for a long time, I lived in the shadowland of daydreams and delusions. I feel like I have now stepped into the sunshine."

Bibliography

Alcorn, Randy. *Christians in the Wake of the Sexual Revolution*. Portland, Oregon: Multnomah Press, 1985.

Bloom, Allan. *Closing of the American Mind*. New York: Simon & Schuster, Touchstone, 1987.

Brand, Dr. Paul, and Yancy, Phillip. *Fearfully and Wonderfully Made*. Grand Rapids, Michigan: Zondervan, 1980.

Brand, Dr. Paul, and Yancy, Phillip. *In His Image*. Grand Rapids, Michigan: Zondervan, 1984.

Briggs, Dorothy Corkille. *Your Child's Self-Esteem*. New York: Doubleday, Dolphin, 1970.

Congo, Janet. *Finding Inner Security*. Ventura, California: Regal Books, 1985.

Conway, Jim and Sally. *Women in Midlife Crisis*. Wheaton, Illinois: Tyndale House Publishers, 1971.

Curran, Dolores. *Traits of a Healthy Family*. Minneapolis, Minnesota: Winston Press, 1983.

Dally, Peter. *The Fantasy Game*. London: Quartet Books, 1975.

Davis, William. *Fantasy: A Practical Guide to Escapism*. London: Sidgewick and Jackson, 1984.

Dobson, James. *What Wives Wish Their Husbands Knew About Women*. Wheaton, Illinois: Tyndale House Publishers, 1975.

Dowling, Colette. *The Cinderella Complex*. New York: Simon & Schuster, Pocket Books, 1981.

Ezell, Lee. *The Cinderella Syndrome*. Eugene, Oregon: Harvest House, 1985.

Glasser, William. *Reality Therapy*. New York: Harper & Row, 1965.

Hayford, Jack W. *Rebuilding the Real You*. Ventura, California: Regal Books, 1986.

Lewis, C. S. *The Screwtape Letters*. New York: Macmillan, 1961.

Lutzer, Erwin W. *Living With Your Passions*. Wheaton, Illinois: Scripture Press, Victor Books, 1983.

Bibliography

Mayo, Joseph L., M.D., and Mary Ann. *The Sexual Woman*. Eugene, Oregon: Harvest House, 1987.

Peck, M. Scott. *People of the Lie*. New York: Simon & Schuster, 1983.

Penney, Alexandra. *How to Keep Your Man Monogamous*. New York: Bantam Books, 1989.

Petersen, J. Allan. *The Myth of the Greener Grass*. Wheaton, Illinois: Tyndale House Publishers, 1983.

Ryken, Leland, editor. *The Christian Imagination: Essays on Literature and the Arts*. Grand Rapids, Michigan: Baker Book House, 1981.

Shedd, Charlie and Martha. *Celebration in the Bedroom*. Waco, Texas: Word Books, 1979.

Sheehy, Gail. *Pathfinders*. New York: Bantam Books, 1982.

Sheehy, Gail. *Passages*. New York: E. P. Dutton, 1976.

Singer, Jerome, and Switzer, Ellen. *Mind Play*. Hempstead, U.K.: Prentice-Hall, 1980.

"The War Within." Appearing in *Leadership Magazine* (Christianity Today, Inc.) Volume III, Number 4 (Fall 1982).

Index

Index

Index

Index

Index

Index

Index

ABOUT THE AUTHOR

Mari Hanes is a popular author and speaker. Formerly executive editor of *Virtue* magazine and current contributing editor, she travels extensively speaking to women across the country about marriage and family. She lives in Bend, Oregon, with her husband and three children.